THE JAPANESE /
THE BODY, M

KINTSUGI

·

GOLDEN JOINERY LIFESTYLE

By Hinata Kobayashi
All rights reserved.

2

Copyright

Hinata Kobayashi
© Copyright 2020 - All rights reserved.

This document is geared towards providing exact and reliable information with regard to the topic and issue covered. The publication is sold with the idea that the publisher is not required to render accounting, officially permitted, or otherwise qualified services. If advice is necessary, legal or professional, a practised individual in the profession should be ordered.

From a Declaration of Principles which was accepted and approved equally by a Committee of the American Bar Association and a Committee of Publishers and Associations.

In no way is it legal to reproduce, duplicate, or transmit any part of this document in either electronic means or printed format. Recording of this publication is strictly prohibited, and any storage of this document is not allowed unless with written permission from the publisher. All rights reserved.

The information provided herein is stated to be truthful and consistent, in that any liability, in terms of inattention or otherwise, by any usage or abuse of any policies, processes, or directions contained within is the sole and utter responsibility of the recipient reader. Under no circumstances will any legal liability or blame be held against the publisher for any reparation, damages, or monetary loss due to the information herein, either directly or indirectly.

Respective authors own all copyrights not held by the publisher.

The information herein is offered for informational purposes solely and is universal as so. The presentation of the data is without a contract or any guarantee assurance.

The trademarks that are used are without any consent, and the publication of the trademark is without permission or backing by the trademark owner. All trademarks and brands within this book are for clarifying purposes only and are owned by the owners themselves, not affiliated with this document.

Disclaimer

All intellect contained in this book is given for enlightening and instructive purposes as it were. The creator isn't in any capacity responsible for any outcomes or results that radiate from utilising this material. Worthwhile endeavours have been made to give data that is both precise and viable. However, the creator isn't oriented for the exactness or use/misuse of this data.

5

Table of Contents

Copyright 3

Disclaimer 4

Introduction 9

CHAPTER 1 – Kintsugi 10

    From damaged to attractive 13

    The Art of Healing 18

    Kintsugi and Anxiety 20

    How Scars Beautify And Also Join Us? 23

    Load Your Fractures with Gold 24

    Your life and your heart 26

    Unpleasant Feelings 28

    Just How to Recover Psychological Pain 31

CHAPTER 2 - Various form of pains 37

    Reasons for Psychological Agony 37

    How To Surge Over and take Advantage Of Emotional Misery? 40

    Launching Deep Emotional Pain 42

    Getting recovered from trauma 51

    How to provide guidance to your heart from emotional pain. 58

    Exercise Self-Care 61

CHAPTER 3 - What is pain? 73

    Pain regulation 75

    Imagination/Innovation as a Treatment. 78

CHAPTER 4 - Recovering our heart with education and learning 82

Assessing and picking up from your pain.................. 90

Moving on with your life after broken. 101

CHAPTER 5 - Reparing all our body, soul and heart damages... 107

Stay clear of beating yourself up............................... 117

Keep favourable to maintain your power................ 119

CHAPTER 6 - Fixing damaged self-confidence........... 122

CHAPTER 7 - Fixing love... 129

CHAPTER 8 - How to repair a heart after beign broken. 136

CHAPTER 9 - Healing with nature 141

Can nature actually make you better?..................... 143

How You Can Get In Touch With Nature............... 150

CHAPTER 10 - Repairing your joy 154

Conclusion.. 160

Introduction

Tale has it that the craft commenced when Japanese shogun Ashikaga Yoshimasa sent his favorite tea dish a chawan that was fractured back to China for fixing. Upon its return, Yoshimasa was displeased to discover that it had been fixed with unattractive steel staples. Plainly this was less than aesthetically pleasing. The shogun instantly tasked Japanese craftsmen to come up with an alternating, more pleasing approach of repair service, and hence kintsugi was born.

The belief is that things are more valuable and stunning, with its background exposed. Imagine a globe where we could embrace our background, simply put our injuries, and discover ourselves and each other even more gorgeous.

CHAPTER 1 – Kintsugi

I consider Kintsugi when I consider my very own brokenness. Like Yoshimasa's dish, I also have been barged in several ways. A few of the scar on me come from my childhood years when I fought with the pain of my daddy's alcohol addiction and from moving a lot and feeling insecure and also scared each time I began a brand-new institution. What are the causes of your very own splits?

I, in some cases, consider myself a metaphorical dish of cracks and afterward, I attempt to visualize that my fractures are now lined with gold, like Yoshimasa's dish. As I picture these gold lines, I recognize they not just inform the tale of my pain. However, they are also the story of my resilience. It is due to my scars that I have actually found out how to recover the pain. Pain is that voice in our head that tells us we are not good enough.

Embarrassment welcomes us to hide our marks. But I have actually discovered that as opposed to hiding this embarrassment, recovery actually comes with owning our stories and also sharing them with others. Our point of scar, our pain in life are not something we should be hiding from the world. We are who we are due to our marks and also not even with them, and a very vivid and sordid piece of our past belongs to what will make us special. I might see myself as a victim, who had a youth filled with numerous problems, and a result is destined to break my whole life.

I need to be extremely conscious to stay clear of these tendencies. However, my own tale has likewise led me to have lots of positive character strengths consisting of compassion, selflessness, approval and also a flexible spirit. And so even though I wish I could have stayed clear of the pain of my childhood years, I understand there have actually been lots of presents that have emerged from my struggles.

Henri Nouwen describes those on the journey of healing their pain as "wounded healers." I am an injured healer. I am a cracked dish repaired with gold lacquer. I am solid in my broken places. My marks are beautiful, and also your own is too. We don't have to maintain concealing our brokenness.

The process of placing the gold lacquer on the cracks does not occur overnight. It going to take some precious time before our scars can be healed. As so, we require to be grace-filled with ourselves and with one another and provide individuals area, time, and support as we all participate in the spiritual process of Kintsugi.

In Japan, kintsugi is the old art of fixing what has been damaged. Pieces of a dropped ceramic bowl are scooped up and put back together; mended using lacquer cleaned with powdered gold that leaves the repair noticeable. The revitalized ceramic ends up being a sign of frailty, stamina and appeal.

But now, kintsugi, which converts as "gold joinery," is the most up to date way of living pattern promising to change our lives. It is unrealistic to expect life will constantly be wonderful. It's unavoidable that, also, when taking the utmost care, breakable things, such as our preferred mug, will periodically break. Furthermore, most of us experience disease, catastrophe and also the loss of enjoyed ones. Hardship is a collateral component of living.

By being planned for the unpreventable, when tough times happen, we can use kintsugi. Rather than sweeping our issues under the symbolic carpeting, we can place ourselves back with each other in a way that embraces the obstacles we have encountered as a component of our life's trip while acknowledging that it is our marks that make us strong.

Recovering our wounds with gold.

The Japanese have a remarkable ancient practice of healing busted porcelains with gold filled resin. The origins of this method originated from the tale of a wealthy man who broke his precious teacup. He sent it bent on to be repaired and also to his awe, and it was returned stapled together. It was unsightly to his eye and pointless. To please the man, a craftsman found a way to repair the mug using gold resin, making it extra gorgeous.

The belief is that things are more valuable and stunning, with its background exposed. Imagine a globe where we could embrace our background, simply put our injuries, and discover ourselves and each other even more gorgeous.

Externally we understand that we grow through our wounds. Though deep inside, we are informing ourselves of a really different story. It is the tale of pity. We keep our wounds concealed away from others, and we conceal them from ourselves too. If we don't look, we can pretend they are not there. If we convince ourselves the wounds are not there, we do not have to confess our pain. Confessing our pain makes us prone.

From damaged to attractive

Witnessing the virtuosity of Kintsugi, one can immediately see its transformative power. Shattered pieces of a pristine vase are skilfully re-joined with gold-laced epoxy to develop a stunning masterpiece and to evoke an interesting question. If such impressive charm can arise from the fragments of a smashed vase, could a comparable improvement likewise be possible with the components of us we believe are ruined beyond repair?

Making the Difficult Feasible.

Kintsugi's first essential technique is to allot our self-defeating psychological verdicts, the "tales" we've built regarding how impossible it is for us to recoup from our devastations, dishonesties and losses. However, to launch the financial investments, we have in maintaining our lives damaged as a suggestion of just how we have actually been unfairly dealt with, used, or abused.

And even a lot more damaging, our tendency to cling to misfortunes as a means to show to ourselves and others that we are "harmed goods," not worthy of love, acknowledgment, or success. The master artists can just take part in Kintsugi's transformational procedure if they concentrate on what is possible instead of on what is impossible.

Preparing the Medium of Adhesive

The 2nd necessary technique of Kintsugi is to prepare the golden epoxy for loading the fractures and also re-joining the shattered pieces of our lives. A great equilibrium of ingredients is needed. If we include way too much gold to the blend, the joints will also be soft to fuse our emotional pieces back together. Yet if we add excessive epoxy, the glue bond ends up being too breakable to develop a permanent bond.

The "gold" in the example represents our desire to be recovered, excessive need, and we established ourselves up for unfinished assumptions. Relocating also quickly, assuming we are recovered and placing too much confidence in powers past our very own capacity, are traps to avoid as we prepare the golden adhesive for our change.

The "epoxy" in the example represents our attachment to positive reinforcement or to our expectation of how swiftly we ought to be proceeding. Being too connected to just fast and also positive activity threatens our determination to accept setbacks. Not just have to be open to setbacks, we need to stay open time and again until what is bonding back right into integrity within us has actually had enough time to "cure." Yanking on items of our newly stuck psychological fragments prior to they have actually had time to integrate is reckless for obvious reasons.

Re-call all the Broken Piece.

The third necessary practice of Kintsugi is to re-experience every damaged piece within us as we take part in our repair process, so we understand their specific shape, placement and feel. Every single item has to be returned to its initial placement within our psyche if we are to change ourselves from damaged to beautiful. Every sharp fragment of destroyed trust, faith or treatment needs to be thoroughly handled to avoid getting cut once again.

But we should agree to touch and also really feel each of them with the "hands of our heart," so we understand them thoroughly and can approve them all right into our new life which is already painted beautifully. This is not a process of indulgence, dramatizing the past, sympathizing with ourselves, or criticizing others, however rather a spiritual process of re-experiencing the pieces of our mankind that make up our greater, more powerful, and gorgeous self.

While we might have been so deeply injured that we never wish to review our injuries and also pain, by having the guts to do so, we find that while our identification might have been broken, we are a lot more than our identification we are a spiritual container for the web content of our lives, a "vase of opportunity" that stands proud and whole as a flourishing testament to the elegance, grace, and durability of the Human Spirit.

How do I understand that the Scars Are Okay?

I used to resent my wounded areas. That wounds can really come to be the locations where we are the greatest, the location where the pain does the holding together. That there is no man-made rush toward healing and hiding of disfigurement, but a permanent, also lovely, recognition that the injury is here to remain.

The understanding that the extra damaged fractured or damaged things are, the much more priceless it is that the damage and repairing are a fundamental part of the story. And also, many shatteringly that the ruined being surrendered itself to allow an additional hands to take care of and recover and an adhesive back with each other.

Kintsugi, with its obvious gilding, always obtains me thinking in a good way regarding the split and fixed locations in my life that are more lovely for having been broken. The breaking part was awful, and also, the marks were painful as they created. However, after years of trying to heal the damage put on my own, I assume I am beginning to realize that it is precise with those torn locations that light and recovery go into, and also new things can begin.

The Art of Healing

The damaged things get revitalized with gold patches. The busted component is truly approved and also valued as a background of the item, a kind of art, instead of getting camouflaged with spotless repairing. With Kintsugi's frame of mind, when things are broken, we do not analyse exactly how it broke. We see something is broken with no judgment. We accept things as it is. We see a shining opportunity to re-create these things with gold.

The history of damage will certainly shine as though celebrating that it still exists much more magnificently. The art of Kintsugi is healing, recovering our minds and our hearts from the occasion and transforming to something greater. The busted component will never be diminished neither camouflaged, and it stays as a scar but as a gorgeous distinct style that exists only one in the world.

When we can welcome all as it is without any kind of judgment, with our heart in tranquillity that is the recovery. We heal our inner self, and the external world, will also be healed. We tend to hide our problems, wounds, busted components, as we are programmed to define with the negativity. But once we courageously approve the reality and welcome as they are, without including any judgment and an objection, like lighting them up with gold, our old pain will certainly become a special radiating form of art, which we will certainly start treasuring. Our pain becomes love, and we will certainly become a lot more caring for others as well.

Healing the Marks of Substance abuse

Whether we admit it or otherwise, drug abuse harms the psyche. However, there is hope in healing to staunch those wounds, and come out even more powerful than in the past.

Dealing with Wounds

On the whole, Japanese culture succeeds in resolving the not-so-sexy facets of the human condition. Isolation, sadness, psychological scarring all of it takes front and the spotlight in a number of their art types. It's a perspective we ought to appreciate in us since we so commonly let our machismo get in the way of recovery. Yet pretending that trouble doesn't exist is no other way to fix it.

Frequently, we see such repression leads to relapse when handling people that have a problem with chemical abuse. A specialist's work is to give clients the devices to challenge their injuries. This recovery procedure mirrors the idea of "golden repair service" located in the art of kintsugi. It requires time and dedication to be successful at healing. Yet equally as any kind of trip worthwhile cannot be completed in an afternoon, the staying power of a sober lifestyle through healing is worth it.

Strength of Scar Tissue.

Looking at your very own inefficient habits straight in the eye? It injures, yes. It's uncomfortable. Acknowledging our issues endangers to compromise our feeling of self. Yet equally as kintsugi gold must reach its melting point before it can be utilized for repairing shards of busted pottery, our psychological wounds have to be dressed properly and be given lot of attention before they can healed.

Kintsugi and Anxiety

Exactly how is this pertaining to clinical depression?

In order to truly get rid of feelings of clinical depression, we at first have to recognize them. The current death of actor Robin Williams advises us that a challenging mind is often a fantastic mind. In order for a person to achieve their best viewpoint and understanding in life, they might initially have to experience serious disadvantages.

Inevitably, what can be a consumer and debilitating problem, when treated correctly, can encourage a victim to become the very best version of themselves, displaying their splits and also using them with satisfaction.

Exactly how can counselling aid?

The idea of looking for coaching, psychiatric therapy, or CBT is to assist you in living a much more satisfying life. It enables you to show, accept, and progress, encouraged by ownership of your sensations, reactions and activities. We like the analogy of kintsugi since it demonstrates accepting the 'damage' we have actually been created and transforming it into a favourable.

Our team believes that with the best assistance, any individual who has experienced the helplessness, misery and the loneliness of clinical depression and associated psychological health issues can live a more satisfying life and utilize their experiences to create a higher human understanding and awareness.

When we accept our troubles and also take possession of them, we become an extra powerful individual, able to be in control of our current circumstance and our future. The very thing that is our downfall can make us stronger, brighter, and extra refulgent than in the past.

Precious scars

Life can be extremely unjust, and also when it is tipped to merely stroll 'on the sunny side of the street' appear impossible and attempt we say. Bashing the suggestion of 'positive thinking' is typical, but it has resulted in the branch of psychology referred to as favourable psychology coming in for likewise harsh criticism.

The second wave of favourable psychology

Not to be perplexed with the superficial 'pop' psychology that is a staple of everything from the way of living magazines to podcasts and television shows, positive psychology is a reputable area of study. Extensively it is the study of human stamina that produces an enjoyable, engaged, and meaningful life. Right here, broken pottery is not fixed in a way that hides the joins. Rather the restoration is made evident, frequently utilizing gold-colored adhesive to highlight what are called 'priceless scars.'

The philosophy is that heartache, errors, and failure become part of life. When we pick ourselves up, we ought not to seek to mask the challenges we have actually faced. We should not really feel obliged to show a perpetually warm disposition and also behave as if they never ever happened. Instead, we acknowledge them and recognize our strength and also what we have actually learned in much the same way that the Japanese celebrate the repairing of damaged ceramic.

How Scars Beautify And Also Join Us?

Every mark, whether noticeable or invisible, tells a story. These marks of life can represent tiny accidents from individual carelessness, show success from battles, or triumphs over obstacles such as getting over a hill climb or running a race. These kinds of marks become part of the trip, the expense of living, of having adventure and opportunity.

However, not all marks are pointers of the greatest moments of our lives. For many, scars are tips of dark times that we often attempt to hide or neglect. Whether visible or unseen, these scars can be a suggestion of the times that left us really feeling damaged. Scars, however, do not need to be causing or shocking. They do not require to leave you really feeling broken or tainted. As the Japanese art kind known as Kintsugi educates us, marks can be strengthening and unifying, and they can symbolize healing and also survival.

In Japanese society, when something like an item of ceramic or porcelain breaks, instead of throwing out the broken items, the artist repairs the fragments along with precious metals such as gold, silver, or platinum. The procedure strengthens the thing, making it stronger than previously. The result is a one-of-a-kind and magnificent piece that is even more lovely and also tougher to damage than the initial.

Load Your Fractures with Gold

Tale has it that the craft commenced when Japanese shogun Ashikaga Yoshimasa sent his favourite tea dish a chawan that was fractured back to China for fixing. Upon its return, Yoshimasa was displeased to discover that it had been fixed with unattractive steel staples. Plainly this was less than aesthetically pleasing. The shogun instantly tasked Japanese craftsmen to come up with an alternating, more pleasing approach of repair service, and hence kintsugi was born.

They say the educator shows up when the pupil prepares, and obviously, this was the correct time as this message was crucial in my forward trip to health and integrity. A lot had occurred in my life that there is inadequate space below to share, even much less to wish others would completely comprehend and understand.

My whole life up until this minute had actually been about getting over one trauma after one more that there were days I would certainly wake up questioning when the following footwear will go down, and also ask God (once more!) why it must be me.

After that, I am advised that when I entered into this globe and also was asked by God what I desired to experience in this lifetime, I had innocently examined the box significant "growth" and disregarded the one significant "stability.

So this present, still wonderfully wrapped in its initial wrapping fabric called furoshiki, appeared in my life besides this while as I ultimately located time to go through and also unbox a couple of remaining boxes of personal belongings accumulated throughout the years among those psychological trips I was forced to take while saying goodbye to a part of my life that was no more serving my greater purpose.

As I opened up the present for the extremely very first time, I was introduced to the loveliest piece of art a jade dish with golden blood vessels going through it. A note inside the bowl read: "Might you become a Kintsugi Master."

Taking a look at the jade bowl, I had an extensive awakening that it was time to bring all the spread items of my previous with each other, and just like this dish, piece them together and end up being whole once again. I believed, "Is this where I'm leading? To understand my life through the art of kintsugi and master the procedure," I believed so. I also think that there are no crashes in life.

Deep space is perfectly orchestrated. It sends out the right people and also exposes occasions at the excellent minute, all appearing in our lives at the most precious time. The message was really clear. To come to be a master of this art, I had to gain from the master himself.

I know this journey I will take is part of the Grand Plan, and that my instructor also has actually been sent into my life by the World. Isn't that impressive? Synchronicity is an effective sensation certainly, and whenever I have actually experienced synchronicity, and I have had a going along with the sensation that some poise went along with it.

Your life and your heart

This process does not try to fix what was broken merely. Instead, the objective of Kintsugi is to make what was damaged much well than new to make it extra stunning than previously. Every Kintsugi reconstruction is different, special, and also has its very own tale to tell. The procedure is not quick. Some repairs take weeks if not months to complete relying on the seriousness of the brokenness, but the outcome deserves the delay.

Have you ever needed God to do a little Kintsugi repair in your life and with your heart? Do you obtain caught paying attention to the lies that swirl around and whisper to you in your weakest minutes: you are broken and also can never ever be healed; you will certainly never ever be enjoyed the method you are; no one will certainly accept you; you aren't wise enough, pretty sufficient, rich enough; you aren't enough. It is typically currently that we shed our grip and everything comes crashing down, making us really feeling ineffective, forgotten, shamed, denied, smashed and irreparable.

I have some good news you see similar to during the process of Kintsugi where absolutely nothing is as well busted that cannot be dealt with and made whole, and we are never busted, also ruined, and surprise, excessive of a misfit for repair, stunning remediation, and wholeness. This wholeness is not instant excellence, neither a serene, comfortable life. Our wholeness is a journey and process that starts with our acknowledgment that we are in the hopeless need of God to get the busted pieces of our life and also do a little Kintsugi remediation.

It is necessary to comprehend that even if we acknowledge our requirement for God doesn't suggest that every circumstance in our lives will be restored right here on earth. The reality is that some marital relationships never ever heal, some individuals never ever damage free from their dependencies, there are times when the loss stays, and the recovery we so desire never comes.

Unpleasant Feelings

Really feeling unpleasant emotions, not remarkably, can be excruciating. This is why many people do not do it. Rather, we overlook our emotions or dismiss them. We attempt to numb the pain with a glass of wine or three. We separate ourselves. We reduced or shed ourselves, or take part in various other sorts of self-harm.

Generally, we count on anything that'll aid us in getting rid of our sensations. "As human beings, we do every little thing we can do to lower our suffering and to prevent pain emotionally. So it is challenging to accept the pain [of our feelings] and also not attempt to do anything to fight it. Several of us learn at an early stage from our guidance that throwing temper tantrums or relying on substances or self-harm is the way to deal with excruciating emotions. Others may be highly sensitive.

Highly sensitive people make up 20 to 30 percent of the populace. They "experience things more extremely, and for that reason have actually had much more difficulties learning to handle emotions due to the fact that they come to be so overwhelmed by them."

However, while we believe we're reducing the pain with our habits, we're actually enhancing it. However, over time, it only increases stress and anxiety: People may experience regret or shame since they're attempting to quit the habits; it can damage their partnerships; their cuts and also burns may call for clinical attention. To put it simply, when we fight the pain: court it, attempt to push it away, avoid it, ignore it, it really activates various other painful emotions, leading to more psychological pain." We also never ever discover healthy methods to deal with. Sitting with our emotions simply implies allowing them, resisting the urge to get rid of the pain, and also not judging ourselves for having these emotions.

Here's an instance: several weeks back, you make agreement with your colleague to socialize. However, she cancels after another buddy gets tickets to see her preferred band on the exact same day. Your sensations are harmed due to the fact that you made these strategies a while earlier, you were anticipating finally catching up, and you seem like you were ditched for a far better deal.

According to experts, you might inform on your own: "It makes sense she would most likely to the performance due to the fact that it's her favoured band"; I'm absurd for feeling pain"; or "I'd most likely do the very same point. Overcome it; you're a child."

However, this only makes you feel annoyed and also mad with on yourself in addition to feeling pain. Rather than judging yourself or battling your feelings, resting with your emotions would resemble this, she claimed: "It makes sense that I'm feeling hurt due to the fact that I was looking forward to hanging out with my friend"; or "I really feel injured that she chose the performance over me, and it's okay that I feel in this manner."

1. Observe your emotions.

Rest very well and observe the feelings you're experiencing without judging on your own. For example, according to an expert, in the above example, this might indicate, stating: "I'm feeling hurt that my friend chose to visit the concert instead of spending time with me. I'm having concerns thoughts concerning what this means for our relationship. I feel like crying, but my throat is tightening up. Currently, I'm noticing that I'm starting to judge myself because I do not intend to weep. This is uncomfortable, but I'm alright; I can tolerate this."

2. Confirm your feelings.

Confirming your emotions suggests approving them. Again, you do not judge your feelings and thereby cause extra pain.

3. Focus on today.

It's also helpful to concentrate our interest on today, rather than "wallowing" in the experience. We wallow when we obsess on the feeling, judge ourselves, or evaluate the individual or circumstance that caused our sensations. We might dwell on the scenario and ruminate concerning the information.

Just How to Recover Psychological Pain

I didn't recognize what mindfulness or the mind-body link was, or that pain = suffering x resistance. All I understood then was the embarrassment and the pain that pierced with me and that my heart was really damaged. I survived, certainly, and also had a few similar experiences ever since. Everyone does. I don't know a single person whose heart had not been damaged at least once.

Over the last two weeks, I saw three of my friends weep as a result of emotional pain. I really felt extremely thankful that they really did not avoid revealing their feelings and opened to me so vulnerably. I truly wanted to make them really feel much better, so I recommended them to check out Kintsugi and see how their scars can be turned to joy.

You observe those physical feelings, explain them thoroughly, follow them, sustain them, and let them be. When I try this awesome art myself for the first time, I was able to notice that I was trying to hurry the procedure. I was discovering the physical experiences in my body and virtually right away trying to remove them somehow, rather than simply being with them. When it was a knot-like experience, I attempted to untangle it. When it felt like a hefty weight on my shoulders, I tried to shrug it off.

When I saw rigidity in my back, I tried to unwind it. I had a terrific instructor next to me, who saw what I was doing and asked me to stop attempting to rush the process. As soon as I surrendered to my sensations without attempting to alter them, I was able to make some progression. After I directed each of my three close friends through this exercise, each of them stated it made them really feel far better, and they now had a method of working through their emotional pain.

The quantity of pain and unpleasantness we are supposed to really feel whenever we have a distressing experience is not infinite. This amount could be substantial when we experience something very impactful, like a person's fatality or a divorce, or maybe a smaller sized quantity of pain connected to less significant occasions, like a mean e-mail from a colleague or a tiny vehicle accident. However, it is limited, and it has an end.

The problem is, when we don't permit ourselves to really feel those unpleasant emotions, we only launch a little bit here and there, so for you to see the route of discomfort is not easy at all. I assume the only means to get through emotional pain is to allow ourselves to feel whatever that requires to be felt as it turns up.

I believe that this concept relates to any emotion favourable or negative. When we are at the top of joy, we remain in that state for a while after that come down. Sometimes memories of the occasion trigger similar emotions, but over time they shed their intensity and, at some point, change into a subtle, pleasant feeling that may get caused by some random idea. Similarly, when we feel angry, it hurts for a bit, and we fume and intend to toss things for a few minutes. Unless we actually allow this sensation to be when it comes up and also give it space to progress, it will certainly keep returning till we are able to provide it the attention it deserves, and release. How to make use of body knowledge to accept and also heal emotional pain:

1. Decide when and also where you will certainly have the ability to dedicate undistracted and also undisturbed focus to on your own. This is necessarily doing it as an afterthought while you are focused on another thing that will not function.

2. When you get to your marked recovery space, do a little ceremony to change from whatever you were simply doing to concentrating on yourself and also your requirements. This event could be fairly easy, shutting your eyes and taking three deep breaths, lighting candlelight, playing a meditation dish, or whatever else makes you really feel extra loosened up and grounded.

3. When you are ready to begin, close your eyes, and remember what it was that triggered the negative feelings. As those memories and feelings, start ahead up, begin noticing the physical feelings in your body.

4. As you pay very close attention to the feeling and observe the physical sensations associated with it, you will certainly observe that after a number of minutes these sensations and emotions might start to alter.

Adhere to whatever your body wishes to do at that moment if the feelings you are feeling are making you intend to snuggle in a ball do that. If the energy is relocating through your body like lightning bolts, follow it and also dance like crazy. If you feel a psychological knot of some kind, see if it intends to be untangled and imagine what would certainly happen if you attempted that. If you seem like crying, cry it out. Just allow these feelings to exist without judgment, observe, and also let them be.

5. If you are into reflection, when you seem like you are done with your recovery experience for that minute, wrap up your session with a loving generosity meditation. When every little thing is going well, it's really very easy to be loving and also type in the direction of myself. Nonetheless, when something happens that makes me question my own "benefits," it's a lot harder. Why isn't there a training course in elementary schools clarifying this simple concept?

However, after I understood what I have actually been doing, I began to react to some negative occurrence in different ways. As opposed to dropping the spiral of self-doubt and evaluating, I began saying to myself, "I like myself when I feel upset" or "I love myself when I feel sad" or whatever it is I'm feeling.

When your heart is damaged, it usually as a result of your demands and assumptions not being fulfilled by another person. Before you can actually receive that love, you need to find out to accept on your own simply the way you are, consisting of all the adverse thoughts and feelings that are gurgling up within you.

CHAPTER 2 - Various form of pains

Psychological Pain And How It Change Us

Agony and also grief is more than simply short-term feelings or passing feelings. Psychological misery has a tendency to influence and also transform the whole individual, from our worth's and expectation of life to just how we deal with others. Understanding how to recognize agony and its results can assist you to carry those changes in a more favourable way.

What Is Psychological Pain?

Pain is a state of serious, usually extended, physical, or psychological suffering. Words pain can be made use of to define the intense pain of either the body or the mind. Psychological misery is a type of serious psychological pain that several of us might experience at some point in our lives, for a brief or an extended amount of time.

Reasons for Psychological Agony

Loss

One of the most usual types of psychological agony is the misery of shedding a person near to us-otherwise, referred to as despair. Practically everyone needs to undergo the procedure of sorrow at some point in life, though for some, pain can strike early and typically.

Mental disease

Emotional misery can additionally come from a psychological and also emotional disorder such as bipolar disorder, anxiety, and also borderline personality condition (BPD). These disorders can create the patient to experience emotional agony a lot more frequently than those that do not have the problem, and also in circumstances where most would not experience high levels of psychological misery (or any type of psychological distress in all).

Physical Illness

Physical pain, whether it is intense (like a busted bone) or chronic (like arthritis), can bring about a state of emotional misery. Persistent pain, particularly, can create a feeling of misery and cause ongoing psychological distress and psychological misery.

Remorse

Previous blunders and remorse's are one more among the main sources of psychological turmoil in life. If you've slipped up that you regret-whether you did something on purpose that you now recognize it to be a wrong act, remorse's can result in prolonged periods of emotional agony.

Being rejected & Failure

Everyone experiences the emotional pain of being rejected or failure at some time in their life. Nevertheless, for some, the sensation of rejection can bring about a relentless feeling of psychological pain that is persistent and also continuous.

Similarities between Psychological and Pain Emotional Pain

We could not be able to make rent this month and also have to borrow cash from our parents or companion, these acute psychological pains are usually rapidly and easily settled (you most likely to function, or you select to stay at home; you obtain the money and settle to pay it back following month).

Psychological pain, on the various other hands, is an extreme emotional pain that is much less conveniently fixed and also much more consistent. Typically, emotional misery does not have a simple solution and therefore lasts much longer. It generally influences us more significantly than psychological pain.

Emotional Pain

A feeling of temper, despair, or negative feeling that has a specified option actually and can be treated through a brief duration or a reasonably straightforward and simple action.

Psychological Misery

Severe psychological pain that does not have an easily-defined remedy and also might just be corrected via a prolonged period or duplicated activities (i.e., therapy).

Exactly How Emotional Agony has some Modifications in us.

Experiencing psychological agony certainly changes an individual; how much is not constantly optional. Nonetheless, we do have the ability to select whether those modifications are positive or negative.

You Safeguard Yourself

Psychological misery can make a person comprehend real importance and fragility of their emotional wellness. You aim to secure on your own from additional emotional misery where possible.

How To Surge Over and take Advantage Of Emotional Misery?

Live In the Moment

We've all found out about the lots of advantages of mindfulness. Yet when it pertains to getting over psychological pain, this truly is one of the primary steps. Residence in the past is the solitary most unsafe thing you can do during periods of serious emotional pain. Instead, concentrate on the here and now and also work on the things you can alter, rather than the important things that run out your control.

Connect

Emotional misery can swiftly cause seclusion, which can bring about also more psychological agony. When you begin experiencing serious emotional pain, one of the very best things you can do, is to make it recognized, whether to a trusted buddy or a therapist. Often, simply claiming the words out loud (or creating them down) to a person that wants to obtain them can take much of the power out of the pain you're experiencing.

Release Blame

Flexible on your own or somebody (or something) that has actually mistreated you is type in overcoming emotional agony. Forgiveness is not just telling us about forgetting what took place, but rather, it has to do with releasing things that you cannot change.

Get Proactive

While comprehending that some psychological pain and even emotional agony is unavoidable, establishing a strategy to create joy in your life, will be good for quick recovery. Frequently, we take happiness for granted and also think that it's something that needs to drop in our lap when as a matter of fact, happiness is something that is very tedious to get except with work and determination.

Seeking Aid with Psychological Agony

While defining misery and just how it alters us forever, emotional pain is just one of the most difficult tests one can get over on his or her very own. Usually, while valuable, the support provided by loved ones is just not enough. Think about producing a far better system for getting rid of agony with the aid of a professional counsellor or therapist.

Launching Deep Emotional Pain

Someone crushed my heart quite badly. It was one of those separations you do not see coming, the sort of heartbreak you never assumed can take place to you. I desired nothing more than to do away with it. So I did. But the only way to heal psychological pain rapidly is by fleeing from it. And also, I understood that it had not been something I can do.

Yet I was so tired of really feeling the pain. I simply wanted it to disappear. We're wired to run from pain. We intend to obtain as far away from it as feasible, whether that means pressing it away or discovering a means to go numb. The problem with those techniques is that they develop larger troubles, in the form of illness, stress and anxiety, and psychological stagnancy.

If you're somebody that wishes to live a deeply fulfilling life, you need to learn to face your pain. I understand it doesn't sound appealing; however, neglecting your pain will only make it even worse in time. Only by looking it right in the face, and also actually taking care of it, can you locate the splendour, appeal, and also pleasure that features true flexibility. Which do you desire for your life?

1. be present with your feelings.

When you really feel an emotion coming on whether it's insignificance, resentment, vacuum, shame, or solitude feel it entirely. To feel your emotions indicates to permit them to develop in the body and notice the feelings that take place. Do not adjust or try to manage them. Permit yourself to be existing and observe them.

Pain sets off childhood years wounds, and we typically revert to versions of ourselves that aren't rational, when we are deeply troubled. It's important not to shame on your own for any type of sensation that comes up, no matter what it is. Treat on your own like you're your own youngster. Tell yourself every little thing is Alright. Tell on your own that you're there. This might seem weird. However, the love we have for ourselves is our greatest device for healing emotional pain.

2. Infuse your heart.

I teach breath work since it's a transformative method for recovery and accessing self-love. There is a selection of means to take a breath that encourages healing. One of the easiest techniques is to rest on the ground and breathe long slow inhalations and also exhalations into the heart. Breathing carefully through your nose and right into your heart can help open the heart chakra, which is usually obstructed when you're experiencing emotional pain.

Breathe this way for 5 to 10 minutes, or longer if you such as. Once again, focus on any feelings that arise and enable them to surface without judgment. You could really feel despair and also the requirement to sob. Don't hold anything in.

3. Howl into a cushion.

I'm a huge follower of screaming. I have my breath work students let out no-holds-barred screams several times during recovery sessions. Using the voice to launch feeling is really cathartic. It assists to push stuck energy out of our bodies and leaves us in a much more peaceful state. Some individuals repress anger for a lifetime due to the fact that they have actually been shown it's wrong or poor to feel rage. It isn't. Even if you do not really feel angry, shouting can be a fantastic energized launch.

So, order a cushion, and shout up until you feel like you're done. If you find yourself needing to weep, let it out. You might really feel a sudden burst of happiness or giddiness, and want to begin chuckling. Whatever you really feel, simply go with it.

4. Move your body.

Our bodies need motion. Attempt playing a positive tune you enjoy and allowing your body action. Nevertheless, it wishes to move. See if you wind up obtaining shed on the track. You may just find yourself experiencing a little pleasure.

In some cases, we remain in a lot of emotional pains that dance simply does not really feel feasible. In those instances, getting outdoors and walking can help raise your state of mind enough to make a significant difference in your day. Attempt some gentle yoga or a walk in nature. Movement obtains power flowing, and aids launch stuck pain.

Keep in mind that humans are wired to look for pleasure and range from pain, so you're most likely not going to be delighted to do any of these things. Do them anyhow. Attempt just one. You'll see a difference in exactly how you feel, and that will certainly be your reward to maintain all your feelings. You will be turning up for yourself, you will certainly be providing yourself love, and you will certainly be healing.

Psychological and also Emotional Injury

If you have actually experienced an extremely demanding or disturbing occasion that's left you feeling defenceless, you might have been distressed. Psychological injury can leave you dealing with disturbing feelings, memories, and anxiousness that will not disappear. It can additionally leave you really feeling numb, disconnected, and not able to rely on other people. When bad things occur, it can take a while to overcome the pain and feel secure again. Yet with these self-help approaches and also support, you can speed up your recuperation. Whether the injury happened years ago or the other day, you can make recovery adjustments and proceed with your life.

What is emotional, and also mental trauma?

Emotional and also psychological injury is the outcome of astonishingly stressful occasions that smash your complacency, whereby you going to feel neglected. Distressing experiences typically involve a risk to life or security, but any type of situation that leaves you feeling overwhelmed and separated can lead to injury, even if it doesn't include physical damage. It's not the objective circumstances that establish whether an event is terrible, but your subjective psychological experience of the event. The more frightened and also powerless you really feel, the more likely you are to be distressed.

Psychological and also the emotional injury can be triggered by:

Single events, such as a crash, injury, or a fierce strike, specifically if it was unexpected or happened in childhood. Ongoing, unrelenting tension, such as living in a crime-ridden area, battling a serious health problem, or experiencing terrible occasions that take place continuously, such as intimidation, domestic physical violence, or childhood years forget.

Typically overlooked reasons, such as surgical procedure (especially in the very first three years of life), the sudden death of somebody close, the breakup of a considerable connection, or humiliating or deeply frustrating experience, especially if someone was purposely terrible

Dealing with the injury of a natural or manufactured disaster can present unique challenges even if you weren't straight involved in the occasion. As a matter of fact, while it's not likely any one of us will ever be the straight targets of a terrorist strike, plane crash, or mass capturing, for instance, we're all on a regular basis pestered by dreadful images on social media and news resources of those individuals who have actually been.

Childhood injury and the risk of future trauma

While traumatic occasions can happen to anybody, you're more likely to be traumatized by an occasion if you're currently under hefty tension tons, have actually just recently suffered a collection of losses, or have actually been distressed previously especially if you re been traumatized during your infant days. Youth injury can arise from anything that disrupts a youngster's feeling of security, including:

- An unsteady or dangerous environment
- Splitting up from a moms and dad
- Serious illness
- Invasive medical treatments
- Sex-related, physical, or verbal abuse
- Domestic violence
- Disregard

Experiencing trauma in childhood can cause a severe and also lasting impact. When childhood years injury is not resolved, a sense of concern and vulnerability rollovers into adulthood, setting the stage for more injury Nevertheless, even if your injury happened years earlier, there are steps you can require to get rid of the pain, find out to depend on and link to others once again, and regain your sense of psychological equilibrium.

Symptoms of mental injury.

All of us react to injury in different means, experiencing a variety of physical and also psychological reactions. There is no "ideal" or "incorrect" means to assume, feel, or respond, so do not evaluate your very own reactions or those of other people. Your reactions are Typical Responses to Irregular events.

Emotional & psychological signs:

- Shock, denial, or disbelief
- Confusion, trouble focusing
- Temper, impatience, state of mind swings
- Stress and anxiety and also concern
- Regret, pity, self-blame
- Taking out from others
- Really feeling unfortunate or hopeless
- Feeling separated or numb.
- Physical signs and symptoms:
- Sleeplessness or problems
- Fatigue
- Being shocked quickly
- Problem focusing
- Competing for heartbeat
- Impatience and agitation
- Aches and also pains
- Muscle tension.
- Recovery from injury

Trauma symptoms typically last from a few days to a few months, gradually fading as you refine the unsettling event. But even when you're really feeling far better, you may be troubled from time to time by unpleasant memories or emotions specifically in reaction to triggers such as an anniversary of the occasion or something that remind you of the trauma.

Whether or not a distressing occasion involves a fatality, you as a survivor have to deal with the loss, at the very least of your sense of safety and security. The all-natural reaction to this loss is sorrow. Like individuals who have actually lost a loved one, you require to undergo a mourning procedure. The following suggestions can aid you to handle the feeling of pain, recover from the injury, and proceed with your life.

Getting recovered from trauma

Try to get moving

Injury interrupts your body's all-natural stability, freezing you in a state of hyper arousal and fear and burning adrenaline and also releasing endorphins, workout, and also movement can, in fact, help fix your nerve system. The exercise that is balanced and also engages both your limbs such as walking, running, swimming, basketball, or perhaps dancing works best.

Ask for assistance

While you don't need to discuss the trauma itself, it is very important that you have someone to share your sensations with one-on-one, somebody that will pay attention diligently without judging you. Look to a relied member of the family, close friend, counsellor, or clergyman. Join social tasks, even if you don't seem like it. Do "normal" tasks with other people, activities that have nothing to do with the traumatic experience.

Reconnect with old close friends. If you've pulled away from relationships that were once essential to you, take the initiative to reconnect. Join a support system for injury survivors. Getting in touch with others that are facing the exact same issues can help reduce your sense of isolation.

Don't separate yourself

Complying with trauma, you might wish to withdraw from others, yet isolation only makes things worse. Attaching to others in person will certainly help you recover, so make an initiative to preserve your relationships and also prevent spending excessive time alone. You don't need to speak about the trauma. Connecting with others does not need to include speaking about the injury.

Ability to Volunteer

Along with helping others, this can also be a fantastic way to test the feeling of helplessness that often accompanies the injury. Advise on your own of your strengths and reclaim your feeling of power by helping others. Make brand-new buddies. If you live alone or much from family and friends, it is necessary to reach out and make new good friends. Take a class or sign up with a club to satisfy people with similar passions, connect to a graduate organization, or connect to neighbours or job associates.

Self-regulate your nerve system

Despite how upset, distressed, or out of control you really feel, it is essential to recognize that you can change your stimulation system and calm yourself. Not only will it help soothe the stress and anxiety associated with injury, but it will certainly also create a higher sense of control.

Conscious breathing.

If you are really feeling disoriented, baffled, or distressed, practicing conscious breathing is a fast method to soothe on your own. Does a certain sight, odour, or preference rapidly make you really feel calm? Or perhaps cuddling an animal or paying attention to music works to soothe you swiftly? Every person replies to sensory input a little differently, so trying out various quick stress and anxiety relief techniques to discover what works best for you.

Take a look around you and select six objects that have red or blue in them — notify just how your breathing gets much deeper and calmer. Enable yourself to feel what you really feel when you feel it. Acknowledge your sensations about the injury as they emerge and accept them.

Care for your health

It holds true, having a healthy and balanced body can increase your capability to handle the stress and anxiety of injury. Obtain lots of sleep. However, an absence of top quality rest can aggravate your injury symptoms and make it more challenging to preserve your psychological equilibrium. Go to sleep and rise at the same time every day and go for 7 to 9 hours of rest each evening.

Avoid alcohol and drugs. Their usage can aggravate your trauma signs and symptoms and raise sensations of depression, anxiousness, and isolation. Eat a healthy diet regimen, Consuming tiny, well-balanced dishes throughout the day will certainly assist you to keep your power up and decrease mood swings. Stay clear of sugary and fried foods and consume a lot of omega-3 fat such as salmon, walnuts, soybeans, and flaxseeds to give your state of mind an increase. Minimize anxiety, Attempt leisure techniques such as meditation, yoga, or deep breathing exercises. Arrange a time for activities that bring you joy, such as your preferred leisure activities.

When to look for specialist treatment for trauma?

Recuperating from trauma requires time, and also everybody heals at their own pace. However, if months have passed and your signs aren't letting up, you may require expert help from an injury professionally.

Look for aid for trauma if you're:

- Having trouble functioning at home or job
- Experiencing serious worry, anxiousness, or depression
- Not able to develop close, satisfying relationships
- Experiencing frightening memories, problems, or flashbacks
- Preventing more and more anything that advises you of the injury
- Emotionally numb and disconnected from others
- Utilizing alcohol or medicines to feel much better.

Overcoming injury can be terrifying, excruciating, and possibly re-traumatizing, so this recovery work is ideal embarked on with the help of an experienced trauma professional. Locating the right specialist may take a while. It's essential that the therapist you choose has experience dealing with trauma. Yet the high quality of the connection with your therapist is similarly vital. Pick a trauma professional you feel comfy with. If you don't feel risk-free, reputable, or recognized, find one more specialist.

Helping a loved one handle trauma

When an enjoyed one has endured an injury, your assistance can play a critical function in their recuperation. Healing from trauma requires time. Endure the speed of healing and keep in mind that everybody's reaction to injury is various. Do not evaluate your loved one's reaction against your very own reaction or any individual else's. Offer useful support to aid your liked one in return into a normal routine. That might imply aiding with collecting groceries or doing household chores, for example, or simply being offered to talk or pay attention.

Do not press your loved one into chatting. However, be offered if they wish to chat. Some trauma survivors discover it difficult to speak about what happened. Do not force your loved one to open up. However, let them understand you exist to listen if they intend to speak, or readily available to just hang out if they don't. Aid your loved one to mingle and loosen up. Motivate them to join the physical exercise, seek out pals, and seek pastimes and also various other tasks that bring them satisfaction. Take a fitness course with each other or establish a normal lunch day with close friends.

Don't take the trauma signs and symptoms directly. Your liked one may become angry, short-tempered, withdrawn, or mentally distant. To aid a youngster recover from trauma, it's important to communicate honestly. Let them recognize that it's normal to feel frightened or dismayed. Your kid might additionally look to you for cues on just how they should react to injury, so let them see you taking care of your symptoms in a positive method.

Youngster's reaction to emotional injury.

Regression.

Numerous kids require to go back to an earlier phase, where they really felt much safer. More youthful children might wet the bed or want a bottle; older children might fear to be alone. It is essential to be recognized, person, and reassuring if your kid reacts in this manner. Assuming the occasion is their mistake. Children younger than 8 tend to assume that if something fails, it should be their fault. Make certain your kid recognizes that she or he did not cause the occasion.

Rest disorders.

Some kids have trouble going to sleep; others wake frequently or have troubling desires.

Provide your youngster a stuffed animal, soft covering, or flashlight to take to bed. Attempt spending extra time with each other in the evening, doing silent tasks, or reading. It might take a while prior to your kid can sleep with the evening once more. Being energetic in a project to stop an occasion from happening once more, creating thank you letters to individuals who have actually assisted, and also taking care of others can bring a sense of hope and also control to everybody in the family.

How to provide guidance to your heart from emotional pain.

Emotional pain is the heartache that arises from experiences such as the loss of a loved one, dashed hopes, and dreams, health problem, injury, clinical depression, stress and anxiety, frustration, fear, sense of guilt and lots of other regrettable conditions. Psychological pain often tends to aggravate when those unpleasant, stressful events are repeated and experienced and also ended up being crippling when they impact mood, partnerships, or specialist life.

Some psychological pain is inevitable. However, a research study suggests that long term durations of persistent emotional stress are carefully connected with a higher threat for heart disease and also sudden death. Researches have actually shown that individuals without spouses on average real-time much shorter lives and individuals that are quick to anger or who show frequent hostility typically run a boosted risk of heart disease. Adverse feelings impact physical health and wellness.

One such problem is Takotsubo cardiomyopathy, likewise called "Broken Heart Syndrome," physiological action to psychological anxiety. It is a kind of non-ischemic cardiomyopathy in which there is an unexpected, momentary weakening of the muscular tissue of the heart. It is clinically various from a cardiac arrest in that prior to the occasion, and the individual had few danger variables for heart problems.

The regular presentation of somebody with Takotsubo cardiomyopathy is an abrupt onset of congestive heart failure or chest pain. Cardiogram changes suggest an anterior wall surface coronary infarction; nevertheless, throughout the course of client analysis, no significant blockages are located; however, a protruding left ventricular peak is usually noted.

The root cause of Takotsubo cardiomyopathy appears to entail unusual feedback to high distributing degrees of catecholamines, likely triggered by adrenaline. It is frequently seen in post-menopausal ladies with a current history of psychological or physical anxiety. Supplied the specific endures their preliminary presentation, the left ventricular function typically boosts within two months, and also, the lasting prognosis is outstanding.

Yet not all emotional stress and anxiety misbehave, and also not all stress brings about the illness. If a sense of control can be preserved over one's life, then tension can be exciting instead of debilitating. By building emotional resilience, we can safeguard our hearts from the adverse effects of psychological pain. The workout is a great way of lowering chronic anxiety, directly lessening the risk of coronary artery disease, and also assisting in managing weight problems.

An additional means is through stress administration programs that typically contain breathing & stretching workouts, yoga exercise, reflection, or massage therapy. There are possibly several other helpful strategies, but they all have the exact same goal to blunt the adrenaline reaction to minor tension. New practices require to be found out to make sure that the "fight-or-flight" reaction is not instantly involved at the first indication of the problem.

Dealing directly with adverse tension and acknowledging psychological injury is the very first step to healing. Therapy alternatives usually include counselling, psychiatric therapy, and cognitive-behavioural treatment. Taking obligation for healing from emotional pain will certainly assist stay clear of living as a target. When clients really feel, they select to act upon reality and to heal. Only after that can they experience the present minute, bountiful life and healthful living. Resolve the past, however, stay in With your family, buddies, and colleagues, and develop your very own future. Be the author of your own destiny and safeguard your heart from the physical wear of psychological pain.

 Exercise Self-Care

1. Exercise great emotional health

Much like we exercise individual hygiene by taking showers and cleaning our teeth, we also require to adopt techniques or routines to deal with our psychological wellness. Here are some suggestions to engage your mental health, proactively avoid mental disorders, and promote mental resiliency.

Address psychological pain.

Bear in mind what experiences in life cause psychological pain for you. Some common feelings that may show emotional pain consist of feelings of pain, temper, rejection, or failing. Although we cannot always regulate the reason for our emotional pain, we CAN practice techniques to treat it. Allowing emotional pain lasts too long can cause clinical depression and other psychological health and wellness problems.

Preserve your self-confidence.

Your self-confidence or level of self-confidence in your capability to complete your objectives has a crucial protective top quality to our mental well-being. It's the lens whereby we see our self-worth from day to day, and also it can impact exactly how we respond to different situations. Prevent letting your self-confidence spiral out of control after an experience of failing or denial.

Have self-compassion! If we let negative life circumstances weaken our self-esteem, we may question our well worth, in turn creating an incorrect sense of doubt that stops us from benefiting from life's possibilities for risk of falling once more.

Avoid recurring adverse thoughts.

Interfere with recurring reasoning or over-thinking regarding distressing or negative occasions in your life by discovering a favourable disturbance. Do something that needs focus to aid prevent ruminating on occasions situations that run out your control or in the past? A cycle of repetitive negative thinking can bring about clinical depression and other clinical issues like cardiovascular disease.

2. Make time for friends and family.

The solitude and also sensations of disconnectedness are severe hazards to our mental health and wellness. Carve out enough time to frequently get in touch with a friend or relative, even if all you can take care of is a call or Face Time session. Taking part in social activities, social tasks like book clubs or group physical education can additionally have a positive result on your mental health and wellness.

3. Make time for yourself

Equally, as we require time with good friends, we also require a time of solitude to be alone with our own specific ideas and sensations. Utilize your time of seclusion to distress from the chaos of life. Take part in activities that you appreciate doing alone like horticulture, checking out an excellent publication, going to the flicks, or food preparation. There are numerous methods to locate solitude for yourself. Require time every day for yourself, and even it's only a few minutes. It's not self-indulgent. It's crucial.

4. Nurture your body with healthy food

Not only does eating healthy and balanced and nutrient-rich foods assist in maintaining your body in good working order. Comply with these three main guidelines to increase your energy and enhance your overall health: Consume plenty of entire foods- fruits, veggies, entire grains, and minimized fat dairy in your food.

5. Obtain enough sleep

Medical professionals advice getting between 7 to 9 hours of rest each night to aid us to perform optimally in our daily lives. As a matter of fact, the absence of sleep due to tension or various other concerns can result in significant health problems. Shut off the displays one hour prior to bed. Utilize this moment to kick back far from the stimulants and prepare your body for sleep.

Attempt to de-stress prior to bed. Lots of hours of rest are lost to agitated minds busied with work or other demanding occasions. Meditate, do some light stretching, listen to comforting music silently, take a warm shower or bathroom. Discover what jobs best to put you comfortable and in a restful state. Exercise previously in the day can aid prepare you for relaxing sleep. Nonetheless, stay clear of extensive exercise right prior to bed.

6. Relocate your body.

To preserve your physical health and wellness, it's currently advised to keep your heart price boosted for at least 150 minutes each week or to get 75 minutes of vigorous workout weekly and obviously, and exercise has other great advantages like increasing your energy, improving your state of mind and helping you go to sleep.

7. Help others.

Occasionally the most effective sensations originate from helping others. Volunteer at your local food bank or soup kitchen area, deal to assist a pal or relative who might need your assistance or give away to your preferred charity.

8. Manage your anxiety.

Stress and anxiety is the body's way of reacting to the mental and also physical demands of life. Common stress factors (occasions or circumstances that create tension) include daily duties and commitments like work, institution, and also household. Often, the trigger for modest to high-stress circumstances includes distressing occasions, the loss of a liked one, health problem, or one more event that substantially changes your life.

Every-day, stress, or short term (severe) tension, can motivate us to focus on jobs, set and accomplish personally and specialist objectives, and can even improve our body immune systems and also shield us from infection.

Alternatively, long-lasting (persistent) tension is the tension of life that wears on for weeks, months, and even years. Persistent stress and anxiety can have hazardous results on our physical and mental health and wellness and can add to or get a worse severe illness like heart problems and diabetic issues and boost the risk for psychological wellness problems like clinical depression and anxiousness conditions. This is why it is essential to discover and also execute tension administration methods to avoid chronic tension.

9. Manage various other clinical or physical troubles.

Are you caring for your medical demands? In times of poor or negative tension or after a significant life event. Mental and physical health and wellness, are deeply interconnected, and it is essential to deal with any type of wellness concerns that might be holding you back. If health issues are a significant life stressor or an element of your clinical depression, take into consideration seeing a therapist who might help you adapt to your new physical fact.

10. Ask for help

You do not need to do anything in life alone. If you're having trouble taking care of yourself for any type of reason, connect. Your medical care doctor can give referrals to therapists or various other doctors that can attend to whatever might be troubling you. Your friends and family can provide assistance and empathy.

How to Stop Adverse Thoughts from Eliminating Your Confidence.

This is perhaps the essential inquiry out there: Just how do you dominate negative ideas that are stifling your self-confidence and bringing you down? You would certainly be amazed to know the solution to this inquiry is much simpler than it appears. Yet even the most basic things can easily drown under the holler and the continuous waterfall of negative thoughts that appear justified. If you could ignore that holler, what would you do? Pursue a brand-new profession, Make new buddies, Take place a date and begin a relationship with an individual who seems unattainable.

To keep reading is to recognize you can do any of these things, and more yet at the same time, this is a dare: to read on is to approve the attempt and select a certain strategy to actions that frighten you.

1. Reveal the Root of Negative Thoughts

Right here's a revelation: Four different studies revealed that people that are unskilled tend to overestimate their capacities blatantly. The research studies gauged wit, grammar, and logic. Individuals who believed they were fantastic were, in truth, unskilled. This shines a light on the origin of your unfavourable ideas regarding your own capacities. As opposed to presuming you're good, qualified, experienced, and born ready to tackle any kind of obstacle, you analyse on your own and also the situation. Previous failings enter your mind.

There's an excellent reason why: very early humans advanced in a hazardous setting. We were threatened by wild animals, natural catastrophes, competing tribes, and also competitors in our very own camps. Our brains are hardwired to look for threat, and when a difficulty occurs, reaction informs us to either battle or flee. You have unfavourable thoughts because your smart mind is considering every one of the possibilities.

2. Emotional IQ

Otherwise known as EI, this is a high quality that goes a long way in the specialist globe, where it's extremely vital for people to have it. We're taught to value the intelligence from an extremely young age. We don't put significantly focus on the capacity to acknowledge emotions and also utilize them inefficient means. It's this lack of balance that leads most of us to stumble.

Adverse emotions trigger unfavourable ideas, and emotion is caused by something you can't regulate. Likewise, the inner verbalization of a feeling occurs nearly instantaneously. You don't also notice when it happens. You really feel depressing due to the fact that you didn't obtain invited to a party. Instantly, you start assuming you're inadequate, and after that, defensiveness begins, and you think, "I don't like those people anyhow."

Also, recognize that the feeling is all-natural, it's wrong or incorrect, it's simply a feeling you have. Be there with the feeling, offer it a name, provide it a shade, and locate a method to reveal it externally. Be innovative, and also, if your expression feels sad, that's because it's authentic.

3. Acknowledge Unhealthy Actions That Reinforce Negative Ideas

We thrive on stimulus. Primarily, this indicates you seek out things to aid you really feel great. A lot of times, when children are really young, parents do them an injustice by supplying a stimulus at the incorrect times. This carries through to adulthood. Unfavourable ideas emerged virtually instantly, like resilient objects on waves of emotion. What's wrong keeping that? The first thing to supply comfort was an outside stimulus in the form of food.

4. Quit Contrasting Yourself to Others

This is a substantial one. It's unbelievably very easy to compare on your own to other people in today's social media sites environment. A research study showed that the more time individuals spend on Facebook, the more clinically depressed they are. Individuals have a tendency to share their achievements by means of standing updates and post pictures that are lovely. It's easy to contrast on your own to your buddies' Facebook façade and show up do not have.

Then, you make a decision to post an upgrade that makes you look excellent, and also, if it does not obtain a lot of sort and remarks, you get the impression your Facebook friends do not like you.

This uses a large amount to individuals that remain in relationships as well. A study showed that when people remain in a major, dependent partnership, they tend to promote it on Facebook.mIf you're not in a gratifying partnership, seeing someone's positive condition in the artificial environment of social networks can be a serious issue.

5. Practice Mindfulness as a Lifestyle

Our Western setting of idea structures things in terms of problems and remedies. It's alluring to claim, "If negative thoughts are the trouble, mindfulness is the service." Mindfulness reflection isn't a solution, and also assumptions for mindfulness creates aggravation. All you can anticipate of mindfulness is to be conscious. It's the method of taking note, and it's the practice of noting sensations and releasing sensations in the same way the lungs absorb oxygen and launch carbon dioxide.

How does mindfulness assist you to cope with unfavourable ideas? The mind bears in mind the idea and, after that, launches it. That's all, and there's no magic right here. There is the acknowledgment that your mind and its thoughts are a working part of an incredible universe. At the danger of seeming motto, a wanderer grows no moss. The mind that releases thoughts and lets them enter deep space does not brood on them. For that reason, that mind remains fresh, and all set for brand-new difficulties.

6. Court Much less, Do More

When we evaluate other individuals and gossip and make adverse remarks regarding them, we give adverse ideas power. With loving-kindness, you sit and guide ideas of well-being and also unconditional love initially to on your own, then to a pal, after that to an associate, and afterward to somebody you do not want.

Next, start documenting particular, attainable check things, tasks, and objectives on your own. Make a note of dates and also areas and get as hyper-specific as possible. Ensure your check things, and also objectives revolve around what you appreciate doing. Keep a laminated duplicate of your order of business in your pocket.

CHAPTER 3 - What is pain?

Pain is "an undesirable sensory and also psychological experience, related to real or prospective cells damages, or explained in regards to such damages." Pain is not simply an easy physical feeling, it is likewise a psychological experience and also needs to be dealt with. Pain isn't constantly related to real damages to the body's cells. It might be brought on by possible cell damages and even simply seem like cell damages despite the fact that none has, in fact, happened. This is described as neuropathic pain.

What triggers the feeling of pain?

Every cell in your body is provided by unique nerve receptors called 'nociceptors.' These are nerves that are specifically made to discover uncomfortable (or 'harmful') stimulations, for instance, severe warmth, mechanical damages like a pinch, or annoying chemicals. When the nociceptors spot an uncomfortable stimulation, the nerve will certainly discharge off an impulse that takes a trip back along the nerve fibre to your spine. From there, the pain message is shared approximately the mind through a spine nerve cell (nerve), taking a trip up via a part of the mind called the thalamus prior to finishing in various locations of the mind's cortex.

The parts of the mind that the pain signals are sent out to be vital due to the fact that they influence the means we regard to pain. For instance, a few of the nerve fibres finish partly of the frontal wattle of the mind, which generally deals with practices and also decision-making. The pain fibres that finish in the frontal wattle trigger us to really feel pain as an undesirable psychological experience, occasionally also creating concern.

On the other hand, the pain fibres that finish in a location called the somatosensory cortex offer what we would certainly consider the simply 'sensory' elements of pain, like its place and also high quality.

Referred pain.

You might listen to individuals discussing 'referred pain.' This suggests pain that initially originates from one body organ or part of the body, however, is really felt in a various location. The commonest instance is the pain of a cardiovascular disease, which might be really felt in the left shoulder and also down the left arm.

Referred pain happens as a result of the method nerves assemble and also interlink in your spine. Deep frameworks such as the heart are provided by various nerves from your skin. In the spine, however, both of the deep and also cutaneous (skin) nerves could meet simply a solitary spine nerve. This indicates that if the heart sends out a pain signal approximately the mind by means of that a person's spine nerve, the mind cannot inform whether the pain originates from the heart or from the location of the skin.

Since a lot of pain signals originate from the skin, and also we just seldom really feel pain from deep body organs, the mind will certainly analyse the signal as having actually originated from the skin, which is where the pain will certainly be really felt.

Pain regulation

Sensitization

Sensitization describes a circumstance where part of the pain path ends up being over-sensitive. Sensitization might happen after extreme, repetitive, or extended excitement of broken cells. When sensitization does take place, pain fibres are most likely to be activated in feedback to stimulations, which would certainly not typically hurt. This might add to the advancement of persistent pain.

Gating

Gating is a regular regulative device that impacts the method we regard to pain. The initial gating device is located in the spine. Right here, regular (non-pain) sensory fibres are connected to pain fibres as though one can subdue the various other. For instance, after stubbing your toe (an uncomfortable stimulation), delicately massaging the skin over the toe (non-pain feeling) can minimize the feeling of pain.

The non-pain experience takes control of and also prevents the transmission of the pain experience. This system is the basis of some sorts of pain therapy, consisting of spine excitement.

Hidden Clinical depression.

I persuade myself they remain in a refuge, someplace I will conveniently keep in mind the following day, the following week. Or the following year. After that, when I require them, I cannot discover them. I can keep in mind the option to obtain them out of my view when they remained in the method or making things look untidy. Yet, when it is very important to utilize them, they have actually disappeared. I have actually placed them someplace where it's as well difficult to discover them.

That's what individuals that experience perfectly hidden Clinical depression (PHD) have actually done. Time in the past, it was essential to store feelings that really did not have an electrical outlet for expression.

I have actually been composing a whole lot concerning PHD and also am presently talking to individuals that think they experience it. The large bulk of individuals I have talked to for my research study have addressed "yes" to this concern: "Did you mature in a household where feelings of unhappiness or pain were prevented, or where you were slammed or penalized for revealing them?"

It appears with PHD that reductions of agonizing feelings end up being established, a routine, and also a lifestyle. It is also most likely that the individual that is doing it no more identifies just how they conceal. Exactly how do you recognize if you're speaking with a person with PHD? They are great at escaping discovery, as they hesitate of the susceptibility and also loss of control entailed.

Yet below, there is extreme despair or rage that has actually leaked down right into the deep recesses of your subconscious. There is hurting solitude behind the grinning face that you think safeguards you. There is stress and anxiety that the globe you're managing will certainly come collapsing down, and likewise, your susceptibility will certainly be revealed. So you understand much more firmly to the photo and "good life" you have actually produced.

The far better the life you have actually appeared to develop, a lot more you can really feel the stress to maintain the exterior. The even more ideal the life others regard you to have, the tougher you might feel you need to function to keep that picture.

It's continuous. Currently, when it would certainly be appropriate and healthy and balanced for you to really feel those sensations, you have a hard time to access them due to the fact that you have actually concealed them away so well. And likewise, they are maintaining you from participating in life completely.

Imagination/Innovation as a Treatment.

Pain can bring about success

As high as we despise it, pain can be an extraordinary incentive. Art, as an example, is something that is typically motivated by extensive and likewise deep suffering, and a few of the most effective operate in the background were developed due to it.

Edvard Munch's paint Scream, as a significant instance, is an expression of pain and irritation as an inescapable part of human presence. It turned into one of the leading ten most preferred and distinguished paints on the planet. Yes, you need to accept life in its totality, pain consisted of.

There are publications and likewise flicks and additionally photos and additionally all type of brand-new types of contemporary art, such as efficiencies, that take care of pain. They have the power to pass through deep right into the artists' and, likewise, the target market's spirits. They irreversibly alter us permanently.

Why is the artist managing these frustrating problems?

As an artist, you are below to reveal on your own, and your jobs work as a mirror to culture. A real artists will certainly not avoid the effective feelings and additionally experiences, of whatever kind they may be. There, nonetheless, is an additional vital part of this too. Artist makes use of art as a method of dealing with their most extreme feelings. They intuitively pick up that they require to refine these sensations, and they do it with imagination.

Most of the jobs substantiated of pain are amongst one of the most prominent, seriously well-known, and likewise popular art pieces. This is so since all of us have these sensations, and most of us experience losses and additionally aggravations and likewise enduring. An artist's provides us a valuable possibility to deal with complicated feelings and likewise refine them with the help of art.

End up being an artist

Yes, you can. Yes, you do have it in you. All of us have it in us, and we are all innovative mammals. It belongs to what makes us human. Locate your type of expression and recognize that there can be several. Are you a garden enthusiast, a chef, a baker, a researcher? There is a great deal of chance for creative thinking in every call in every leisure activity. Where do you find yourself? What types come simply to you, what are you normally proficient at? What attracts you, what appears to be calling you? Art is liberty, and you can develop art, making use of most anything. Utilize it, do it, share it, change it.

Change the pain.

Possibly not a worldwide distinguished work of art, however, you can develop something that will certainly aid you to endure and make it through everything.

Tips for Dealing with Loss.

Remember that you are, keep in mind that you belong to nature, which in nature, absolutely nothing is irreversible. Fatality, loss, and devastation belong to life, an inescapable part of life that requires to be welcomed and approved. Staying in our greatly technical culture concentrated on marketing us impressions, the suitable variations of 'excellent' life as lacking the fact as feasible, has actually maimed and waned us right into an incorrect feeling of privilege as opposed to humbleness when faced with Nature and its strength of devastation that can just be matched by its capability to develop life.

We have a lot to pick up from the old societies of the East when it involves recognizing nature. They were far more harmonic with it than our culture has actually been for the last century. As quickly as one is birthed, one is currently punished for fatality. As my friend did say, 'life is a temporal illness.' The faster we realize and discover to approve this truth, the far better. Just by approving fatality as an unpreventable part of life, one begins to live totally.

CHAPTER 4 - Recovering our heart with education and learning.

Geometry and History, English, and scientific research locations and times for these topics in the modern class are safe and secure. Yet the heart? Aren't we concerns about the heart personal spiritual issues that are best left in your home? If so, a person had better inform the kids. While we grownups remain to discuss these concerns, a lot of pupils remain to bring their hearts to college.

Comprehending heart education and learning.

When a heart exists in education and learning, interest changes, as the top quality of interest changes, we pay attention with wonderful treatment not just to what individuals claim yet additionally to the messages in between words tones, motions, the flicker of sensation throughout the face. and afterward, we focus on what has heart and definition. The yearning, marvel, knowledge, concern, and complication of trainees end up being main to the educational program. Concerns end up being as essential as solutions.

When the heart gets in the class, masks slope, pupils risk to share the delight and abilities they have actually been afraid would certainly prompt envy is also their buddies. They take the chance of subjecting the pain or pity that peers could evaluate as the weak point. Seeing deeply right into the point of view of others, approving what has actually felt not worthy in themselves, trainees find concern and start to learn more about mercy.

The body of the kid will certainly not expand if it is not fed; the mind will certainly not prosper unless it is boosted and directed. And the spirit will certainly endure if it is not supported. An emotional education and learning welcome varied methods to please the spiritual appetite these days' young people. When directed to discover positive methods to share their spiritual washings, youngsters can locate function in life, do better in the institution, and enhance connections to friends and family, and method grown-up life with vigour and vision.

Plainly, this is not an esoteric interpretation of heart or spirit. To involve those concerns would certainly take us right into the world of idea and conviction. While completely proper for approach or spiritual education and learning, basing the educational program on any type of specific meaning of heart would undoubtedly split us and breach the worldview of one team or an additional.

Consequently, I utilize words heart to require an interest in institutions to the internal life, the deepness measurement of human experience, to pupils' longings for something greater than an average, product, and fragmented presence.

Can We Collaborate to Address Heart in Schools?

Educators are starting to describe a 'spiritual issue' in our society. Scholars examining college physical violence mention 'spiritual vacuum,' and members of Congress having a hard time for remedies lament the 'spiritual darkness' that affects the young. An agreement is arising that some type of spiritual gap exists for young people, and we have to resolve it.

Normally, our colleges mirror this issue. However, can we encounter with each other the inquiry of beneficial heart in the class, or is it also tendentious to permit us to progress? I think that we are better able to satisfy this obstacle currently than at any moment in our background. On the one hand, the variety of confidences and non-faiths today in a lot of institution neighbourhoods is so frustrating that no solitary religion might potentially be appropriate as authorities, and even informal, college faith.

On the other hand, with also physicists and astronomers participating in the mission for the response to the old-time inquiries concerning the significance of life, instructors can no more claim that outlawing spiritual inquiries from college building is practical. And there is an expanding understanding amongst moms and dads and teachers that a spiritual gap is threatening our young people and our neighbourhoods.

Although we need to deal with the socioeconomic resources of the consistent fierce and suicidal habits of our teens, we cannot actually recognize or recover from these plagues if we do not start to identify and satisfy the spiritual demands of our youngsters. Do we require regular suggestions from sawed-off shotguns to reveal to us that these youths feel? Is it feasible that these ridiculous acts of physical violence are assisting us back to what, in our hearts, we understand a core goal of education and learning to begin with?

Maybe we do require these suggestions. Numerous neighbourhoods determined years ago that the internal life of our youngsters was just not the business of public institutions. Lots of class are 'emotionally vacant,' not by the crash, however deliberately.

We made a decision to leave out the spiritual measurement from education and learning due to the fact that we grownups could not settle on what 'it' was or exactly how to show 'it.' Liberals are afraid that 'diehards' will certainly sue them as 'New Agers' if they present a spiritual measurement right into the class. Christians are afraid that secularists will certainly disable their initiatives to offer spiritual advice to kids in institutions. Various other spiritual teams are typically not also consisted of in the discussion. Jointly, we got to a standoff, and our youngsters have actually lost.

Numerous neighbourhoods have actually made a decision that the internal lives of our youths in the general public institutions would not be any person's organization. Looking for a considerate means to take care of our distinctions, we teachers averted from issues of religious beliefs and spirituality. Obviously, several educators, institutions, and neighbourhoods are committed to offering the social, psychological, ethical, and also spiritual demands of pupils.

Yet when colleges methodically leave out body and soul, pupils in expanding numbers ended up being clinically depressed, effort self-destruction, or catch consuming conditions and drug abuse. Trainees battle to discover inspiration to find out, to remain in institutions, or to maintain their focus on what is prior to them. Pleasant heart right into the class is not a cure-all for all these sicknesses, however, it is vital for dealing with the suffering of our young people.

Up until lately, teachers would certainly have satisfied the topic of this publication mainly with worry that it will certainly reduce the rage of individuals that will certainly damn them, sue them, and eliminate their tasks. Yet something is transforming.

Educators and social researchers are asking, "Exactly how can we fill up the spiritual space?" since they see pupils ruining themselves and each other. Others have actually directly glimpsed the treasures of the internal life in the wave of spiritual search and revival amongst grownups in the 1990s. Both teams are asking, "Exactly how can we suitably resolve our pupils' spiritual development in manner in which do not break the ideas of households or the splitting up of church and state?"

My very own job has actually been notified by two impulses: a wish to avoid physical violence and a wish to recognize the spiritual yearnings in youths. I started my collaboration with teens looking to produce educational programs and approaches that would certainly attend to the source of enduring in a 'generation in jeopardy.' Collaborating with young adults, I additionally found an elegant opening to spirit at the heart of the teen experience.

Teenage years is a time when yearnings stir up with a strength that numerous have actually misconstrued and disregarded as 'hormonal agents.' The bigger inquiries concerning definition, identification, obligation, and function start to push with a necessity and solitude we can all bear in mind. Neglected or subdued, the spiritual pressures inside our young turn harmful and eruptive. Giving pupils with possibilities to funnel their power constructively and to discover their secrets with peers and helpful senior citizens.

Promoting Soul education and learning in Schools.

It is a little yet important action from the education and learning of the soul to The Heart of Education and learning. Absolutely nothing could be extra 'emotion loaded' in a favourable feeling than the experiences that trainees state as beneficial to their Souls. As we encounter this concern, "Just how can we nurture spiritual advancement in the institution?" the areas of social and psychological knowing, brain-based understanding, and knowledge concept have actually been incredibly valuable.

Yet they do not respond to the inquiry. The response does not originate from books, existing studies, or esoteric writing. Instead, it starts in the hearts of the children and ladies, the girls and boys that being in class. For greater than 20 years, my associates and I have actually been paying attention to what youngsters question themselves, regarding each other, and concerning deep space itself.

The internal life of these and various other youths is thoroughly bound up with issues of definition, function, and link, with imaginative expression and minutes of pleasure and transcendence. All these high qualities are main to both psychological knowledge and to constructively loading the spiritual space.

Class atmospheres that recognize and welcome such experiences assist trainees in breaking down stereotypes, boost self-control, boost scholastic inspiration, foster creative thinking, and maintain even more youngsters in the institution. Allow us to risk to think about with each other the opportunities and mistakes of knowingly recognizing in college the internal lives of our trainees.

Assessing and picking up from your pain.

I am really feeling pain, and my eyes are wet, my heart is haemorrhaging, I feel this thickness in my upper body and a darkness that blinds my head", we have actually all felt this spring pain at some time or the various other, be it a break-up, a relationship that is not reciprocated, or a count on that obtains adjusted, a heartbreak is inevitable, yet fortunately is you can conquer it.

Since I remember, I have actually been having a hard time to manage pain, be it my household, good friends, love, death, or desires. By means of managing pain was to obstruct the individual that triggered me pain entirely. This would certainly have functioned flawlessly if those individuals could be totally removed, however, as all of us recognize that's not constantly feasible. In my context, it essentially indicated that if I did not discover to manage my pain, in this life, I would certainly be birthed once again with the very same situations, till I discovered my lesson, which did not seem like a wonderful concept, so I needed to obtain relocating.

As people, high-perceived control makes us really feel much less susceptible to this reason places us in our convenience area. An easy instance would certainly be that we really feel pain, not destruction when we have a busted arm vs. destruction when we have a broken heart, WHY?, There could be two possible answers for this,

1. we comprehend the recovery procedure of a damaged arm much better,
2. healing of a busted arm has a particular extra result than a broken heart.

So I presume it's secure to claim that expertise and assurance of a result necessitates a much less psychological episode. So if we were to use the exact same concepts to psychological "Pain," will it function? In many cases, it would certainly as expertise is a device that produces knowledge, and knowledge is all we require to live a satisfying life.
Your pain can be of different varieties from these;

Social Exemption.
What is a social exemption? Put simply, and it is being omitted type gatherings like birthday celebrations, getaways, workplace gets together, or any kind of such task wherein you have actually been selected and not been welcomed to be a part of the team. The social exemption is an intricate principle and causes

injury occurring out of pity. Pity, although not completely an unfavourable feeling, is still a social feeling, one we really feel when we look negative before others.

Likewise, we often tend to self-incriminate after having actually been left out, either thinking that we in some way deserved it or that we are blowing things disproportionate and should not really feel in this way.

Heartbreak by a fan.

You like a person, and all is working out, and, suddenly, he/she chooses to desert you. What do you really feel pain! .The sensation of Loss is so solid that you can really feel physical misery. You experience highs, lows, sensations of vulnerability, insecurity, misery, due to the fact that the something that you like has actually selected to leave. There is an essential distinction suffering created as a result of separates and various other sensations of loss.

In a "Split," the desertion runs out option and outright, i.e., it is a lot more like a period instead of a comma. Ladies have a tendency to take a bigger strike after a split due to the fact that ladies are socially conditioned to think that preserving a connection was their obligation.

Split really feels somewhat various from various other sorts of loss, and there is an excellent reason. Scientific study has actually verified that coming through heartbreak resembles coming off medications. Lots of researches have actually revealed that the suffering experienced throughout a split triggers the exact same part of the mind that is boosted throughout dependency withdrawal.

Scientists have actually developed resemblances in brain scans of individuals undergoing charming being rejected and drug-food craving. This example of contrasting a heartbreak to dependency might aid you to reason out your heartbreak much better. Just like any other dependencies, the withdrawal signs and symptoms are worst at first, and after that, the signs and symptoms lower.

Betrayal.
Betrayal is when somebody you rely on exists to you, rips off on you, misuses you, or injures you by placing their very own self-involvement initially. Betrayal harms! It's a damaging feeling of loss that causes pain. Some claim it's the awful type of loss any individual can experience as in order to really feel betrayed, you would certainly have relied on the individual, to begin with.

As an example, a partner is betrayed when their companion has an event, and a kid really feels betrayed when mistreated, a close friend really feels betrayed when something specified in confidence is duplicated. Betrayal is an activity of option, and the individual that was betrayed thinks that the option was wrong and avoidable.

Death.

Death results in grief. There is a huge difference between pain and grief. Despair is the psychological-emotional experience adhering to a loss of any kind of kind (connection, condition, work, home, video game, earnings, etc.), whereas grief is a particular kind of sorrow pertaining to somebody passing away. The distinction can be discussed by an easy instance, and when bereaving, we intend to maintain the individual to live in our memories, in time we pick warm memories to the prize.

Nonetheless, when regretting, we attempt to forget or overcome the memories connected to that individual or circumstances by developing brand-new memories.

Understand Your Healing:

It is really crucial to comprehend that the recuperation procedure of each sort of pain is various, differs in strength and time. Some might need simply re-programmed hopefulness, while some might call for additional actions. For instance, managing a

Split might call for staying clear of triggers and proceeding, betrayal might call for a re-connect. Social Exemption might need standing, and Death might need discovering to live once more.

One cannot get rid of psychological memory, and recovery occurs by living an extra wilful life, with re-arranged top priorities and much better expectation. So bellow's just how one can start their trip in the direction of recovery.

Acknowledge Pain

In order to recognize our pain, we initially need to approve. Do not keep feelings after shocking occasions by doubting as to why they needed to occur to me and contradicting that they have actually occurred. You will certainly catch your feelings by contradicting them. Things occur in our lives that aren't reasonable. It draws, and it injures, and there are never ever adequate factors.

Feel Your Feelings Without Judgment:

When you have actually been injured, you might really feel a different variety of feelings like temper, despair, embarrassment, frustration, anxiety, and so on. Allow your feelings circulation without judgment of incorrect or appropriate. This is the challenging component as a lot of us have actually been conditioned for simply the contrary, "do not really feel," "do not weep," "you angle feel by doing this," and so on. Approve that something has actually taken place, allow your body to feel what it wishes to really feel.

There is no right or incorrect sensation, and all sensations must be welcomed with equivalent focus. Do not hesitate to break out sobbing, or shout right into a cushion if you really feel mad and annoyed. These sensations will certainly pass if you reveal them.

Feelings require expression, and subdued feelings cause several problems, which, as most of us recognize, is not a great location to be in. Sometimes individuals experience extreme sobbing throughout their very first reflection method, and I am an initial hand witness to this. Wept unstoppably, I cannot comprehend this in all. I was anticipating this fantastic feeling of calmness, no rips. As it so takes place, arbitration launches all your bottled-up feelings, in some cases, via splits.

In time all the adverse feelings will certainly relocate via you, leaving you with the void, which you can after that purposely fill out with favourable feelings like heat, happiness, approval, and concern.

Concentrate on Self:

Obtain more powerful, mentally, and literally. Attempt to construct a more powerful spiritual framework. I am not speaking about religious beliefs; I am discussing a sounder psychological toughness. Remember, you're feeling of merit does not originate from outside approval. It originates from recognizing that "I suffice." Individuals act as a specific means as a result of their very own desires and requirements.

They might condemn you for their activity to minimize their responsibility, yet that has actually obtained absolutely nothing to do with you. So do not contemplate in unfavourable ideas, believe favourable ideas that will certainly enhance your self-confidence. Check out excellent publications, get in touch with individuals and teams that can match your trip. Know that there is constantly an area for you to radiate and grin, inform on your own sufficient times, aloud if called for.

The endorphins that are launched throughout a workout are infamously useful in raising your state of mind. The workout is the least utilized anti-depressant. Most likely to the health club, do yoga exercise, biking, running, strolling, anything that is literally tough. This is something that you can do on your own where you'll be required to produce a calculated power change from your mind to your body.

This will certainly not just make you literally more powerful, yet it will certainly additionally provide a far better feeling of self well worth. Do something about it:

Foster Fulfilling relationships: It is essential that as we age, and also when all is working out, we make a genuine effort in creating a couple of top quality partnerships that you really feel comfy drawing on. In this manner, also when the sunlight is not beaming brilliant, you will certainly never ever be left without any person to resort to.

Talk It Out: 2 method interaction with the individual that created your pain can occasionally be extremely recovery. Make sure that you concentrate on your very own sensations by claiming, "I really felt" rather than "you made me really feel." Listen to the various other individual bents on obtaining a far better understanding of what occurred, why it occurred, and why it injured. In some cases, things might emerge in different ways. Share your concerns and pay attention to their worries in return. Every person is combating their very own fight, often speaking it out assists place things in viewpoint.

Do not Act Quickly: Wait prior to you make any type of wide choices. There is no favourable vengeance. Retribution in the warmth of the minute is something that you will certainly pertain to be sorry for later on. Time invested in determining a purposeful vengeance is time invested at the cost of your very own psychological recovery.

Take aid: A friend or a specialist can assist you to remove your head and determine what actions to take. If your sensations are as well extreme to handle alone or if you find yourself dealing in harmful means, you need to talk with a therapist that will certainly remain in a much better setting to assist you in managing your feelings.

Forgive: Forgiveness is required in all types of the recovery procedure, leaving apart Death, naturally. Forgiveness results in a better feeling of individual tranquillity. It does not imply that you are ignoring the act itself. What it suggests is that you are picking to proceed from sensations of animosity to sensations of resolution. Also, a tiny case may require to be thought of periodically prior to it quits harming. Forgiveness isn't something you provide for the individual that mistreated you, and it's something you provide for "YOU."

Forgiveness is a procedure and not constantly very easy, and sometimes, it harms greater than the injury itself. Larger pains emerging out of heartbreak or betrayals can specify your life for some time, and it makes good sense that they need to be forgiven numerous times. You can forgive without reconstructing your connections. Actually, in cases of misuse, it is a good idea and occasionally not also risk-free to return to get in touch with.

If you are not able or resistant to return to get in touch with, specifying your forgiveness to on your own or creating it down on a notepad can aid you to carry on from the pain. We never ever recover up until we forgive.

Carry on and Restore Your Life: Restoring is a large action of your recovery trip. Caring a person once again, relying on a person once more, or maybe relying on the very same individual once more, being prone once again, all this can be really overwhelming. Yet life has to take place, and unfavourable cases can not specify you. Open your mind and seek a lesson. Often, the lesson isn't obvious instantly. However, if you maintain an open mind, the lesson will certainly reveal itself.

Moving on with your life after broken.

Feelings of hurt are never very easy or simple to deal with. They are really individual and make us feel unpleasant and useless. Nonetheless, there are specific things you can do that will assist you to lessen these feelings.

Focus on Your Blessings

Nevertheless, things do happen, and as a matter of fact, if you require time to really consider it, there are possibly a lot of things that matter and a lot of things that you can in fact be grateful for. This will hopefully place your feelings right into the correct context. It may also assist you re-prioritize and move your emphasis onto more important and purposeful things that will certainly bring you a greater range of joy and gratification.

Focus vividly on Your Strengths

Locate your direction during the period of hurt, and it is very important that you remind yourself of your strengths and of all the things that have caused it in your life career. Your stamina may come in the form of a positive outlook, belief, persistence, mercy, sincerity, compassion, self-belief, etc. These are the things that will certainly obtain you via this difficult period of your life. Actually, these top qualities can assist you in restoring the self-confidence you require to relocate beyond this uncomfortable experience.

It's as a result, crucial to re-direct your powers far from what's hurting you, and instead redouble on your best top qualities. These are the top qualities that can help you make it through this tough circumstance in ideal means.

Let Go of Past Hurts

Are you keeping things that injure you years ago? Possibly, you're holding onto these injures since you feel as though you were unjustly mistreated somehow. However, what's the factor? Can you do anything regarding these hurts right here, right now? If you cannot, after that, what's the point of keeping them?

This, naturally, doesn't indicate that you ought to ignore whatever that occurred. Actually, do not attempt to neglect these critical moments of your life. Pick up from these experiences and use them to make better decisions today. Nevertheless, don't allow your previous harms to haunt and worsen the life you're living today.

Make an Initiative to Smile More Often.

Being hurt is a state-of-mind. You are feeling hurt because you view occasions, circumstances, and people's objectives in a specific manner in which makes you feel miserable. Is it feasible that one more person might see things a little in a different way? What harms you may not also phase them. It's all a state-of-mind. To transform your state-of-mind, try grinning a bit more and see exactly how that changes you feel about the circumstance. Possibly your feelings of pain will certainly develop into interest and when this happens, an entire brand-new world of possibilities will certainly open for you.

Always Approve Responsibility.

Your pain feels at its worst when you feel as though you had very little control over the scenario. This makes you feel rather powerless and makes it extremely difficult to move past your feelings of pain. One needs to feel better regarding yourself promptly is to approve duty of what occurred and for exactly how occasions have taken place.

As a matter of fact, you possibly somehow figured in creating this situation. Identify this. You are at the very least partly responsible for what occurred, and this is a good idea, due to the fact that with responsibility comes the determination to initiate positive change. As soon as you feel at the very least, this gives you the toughness you require to make things better possibly, to the right the misdoings. You currently have the power to heal your connections and set a course for a more favourable future.

Surround Yourself with Motivating People

Among the very best means to make on your own feel better nearly instantly is to speak about your feelings with other people. Have a conversation with a close relative or buddy and explain what took place. Get their point of view and opinion about the scenario, and perhaps even collaborate with them to try and settle your feelings.

There is no informing how much better you will feel once you get things off your chest. And that understands, maybe the various other individuals can encourage you that there's really absolutely nothing really here that justifies the need to feel hurt. And simply probably that's all you require to help you move on in optimal methods via this period of your life.

Don't Take Things So Directly

You will certainly wind up feeling pain if you remain to take things personally. Occasionally people say and make things due to the fact that they are attempting to work through their own individual instabilities and issues. Actually, what they say and do could have little bit to do with you, and all to do with the issues they're fighting with.

Consequently, it's crucial that you tip "outside yourself" during minutes of pain and look at the full image from their viewpoint along with from an outsider's perspective. Doing so will certainly help you acknowledge that there's nothing actually here to feel injured about. Instead, show a little compassion for the various other individual and try to help them work through their own personal instabilities.

Individuals Make Errors

Sooner or later, somebody will certainly harm you. There's no avoiding this. It will occur. Nevertheless, regularly then not, people will not harm you purposefully. People simply make errors.

Individuals make mistakes and errors, and end up being sorry for some of the important things they do and claim. Of course, they may not own up to these blunders. Ultimately, they will occur and confess their mistakes. However, it may take some time. Be there for them and accept them totally since you might effectively be in their footwear eventually in the future.

CHAPTER 5 - Reparing all our body, soul and heart damages

Fixing Job Loss

In an economic crisis, job losses are inevitable. As for usage and manufacturing loss, firms naturally have to stop hiring besides important staffing demands. Several people may need to dismiss personnel with redundancies, which contributes to an already worrying unemployment situation. It is a vicious circle; as the varieties of those unemployed rises and their revenue drops, consumer investing decreases, which consequently obliges companies to cut back on production degrees, causing even more job losses.

This is not the time to withdraw from your circles. Your network, including your prompt family, relatives, friends, colleagues, former customers, and company contacts, issue now more than ever. Many individuals rely upon word of mouth to locate the right people, so make certain to inform every person you know that you get on the marketplace.

Do not wait till you are pressed. Lots of people completely time employment convince themselves that it won't happen to them wishing they will not be influenced. Nevertheless, if you recognize that it is inescapable that your company or sector is likely to give up individuals and your assessments have actually been of worry, it's finest to start the job search prior to you get the notice.

Establish yourself.

Are there some important skills that you require in order to enhance your potential customers? Do you have the ability to reach where you intend to be? Now, do not scamper to do the very first Master's or Ph.D. program that you obtain admission for; I suggest sensible abilities that all firms need, such as IT or electronic marketing abilities. Consider doing it currently, and you will certainly be much better outfitted with a skill set for your following job.

It is usually taken into consideration that volunteering can have a favourable effect on the look for re-employment. It might not constantly result in paid work. However, it definitely does feature individual and social benefits. The offering will give you a feeling of gratification. It can additionally boost personal capability, present brand-new expertise; all this can help in the look for a permanent role.

Can you speak to me? An employer might need your ability but may simply not be able to manage to employ you as a full-time worker. By offering your skills on working as a consultant basis, you can stay connected to your network and still be well-positioned for an extra irreversible setting when things improve.

There is absolutely nothing more annoying for a potential company than to have the misfortune of reviewing a CV packed with grammatical and typographical errors. Prepare your CV and check it extremely carefully; there are numerous great online examples and suggestions to direct you. Do not make belief to be what you are not; you will certainly be caught out.

Be prepared for meetings.

If you are among the little portion of those that reach secure an interview, you owe it to on your own to be prepared. If you don't understand anything regarding the company welcoming you, maybe embarrassing. Do your study. What worth can you add? Seek troubles to resolve. Prepare inquiries that you wish to ask. There are thousands of individuals searching for work. What makes you one-of-a-kind?

Attempt to stay positive.

Yes, you have actually sent your Curriculum Vitae to 82 firms and talked to with 18; some may not even recognize your CV; it's absolutely nothing individual. They have a lot to go through. Dust off the disappointments as quickly as you can and remain concentrated on the next possibility. If you are down and dejected, it will reveal and can make you show up unappealing. You require to be upbeat, passionate and be positive.

Be adaptable.

Do not be as well fixated on getting your desired job. Be prepared to accept a role that may not necessarily satisfy your expectations when you consider your credentials, know-how, or your experience. Part-time or agreement work are ways of getting you used if you prove to be an outstanding source. There are many ways too many people browsing, so if you are used something that you can do well, approve it whilst you proceed with your search.

Keep healthy and fit.

Especially if you are worried or distressed, your health can be affected, so do not disregard this crucial aspect of your life. All of us recognize that a healthy diet regimen and workout benefits the mind and body. You have the moment currently to offer some emphasis to this, so put an appropriate routine in place. It will put you in a much better state of mind as well.

Why is job loss so demanding?

Our jobs are much more than simply the means we make a living. They affect just how we see ourselves, in addition to the method others see us. They give us structure, purpose, and meaning... Beyond the loss of revenue, shedding a job likewise features various other significant losses, several of which may be much harder to encounter:

- Specialist identity
- Self-worth and confidence
- A daily regimen
- Purposeful activity
- A work-based social media
- Your sense of security

Regardless of just how devastating your losses seem right now, you future can still be bright. With time and the best coping strategies, you can come to terms with these setbacks, alleviate your stress and anxiousness, and carry on with your occupation.

Grief after job loss

Grief is a natural action to lose, which includes the loss of a job. Losing your job forces you to make quick adjustments, which can leave you feeling upset, angry, clinically depressed, or out of equilibrium. Provide on your own time to adjust. Regretting the loss of your job and getting used to joblessness can take time.

Think about your job loss as a momentary obstacle.

Several individuals who make it to the top today have battled a lot difficulties in the past before reaching their promise land. However, they have actually turned things about by selecting themselves up, gaining from experience, and attempting once again. You can do the same. Discussing your loss in a journal, as an example, can help you to look reasonably at your new situation and put things into perspective.

While every person grieves in different ways, the following coping pointers can assist you in managing both the mourning procedure and the stress of your job loss in a healthy and balanced means.

Reach out to stay strong

Your natural response at this tough time may be to take out from loved ones out of embarrassment or shame. However, do not ignore the importance of other people when you're confronted with the stress of job loss and unemployment. The social call is nature's antidote to stress. Nothing works better at soothing your nerves than talking in person with a great listener.

The individual you talk to doesn't have to be able to use remedies; they simply have to be a great listener, somebody that'll listen diligently without ending up being distracted or passing judgment. And making a significant distinction in exactly how you feel, connecting to others can help you really feel much more in control of your scenario, and you never recognize what changes will occur. You might intend to withstand requesting assistance out of pride, yet opening up won't make you a burden to others.

In fact, lots of people will be flattered that you trust them enough to rely on them, and it will just strengthen your partnership.

Creating brand-new partnerships after your job loss.

It's never too late to expand your social media. It can be important in both helping you cope with the stress of job loss and unemployment-- and locating new work. Construct brand-new relationships. Meet new individuals with typical interests by taking a class or signing up with a group such as a publication club, supper club, or sporting activities team.

Join a job club.

Other job seekers can be vital resources of support, support, and job leads. Being around others encountering comparable difficulties can aid energize and encourage you during your job search.

Volunteer.

While joblessness can wear on your self-confidence, offering assists, you keep a feeling of value and function. And helping others is a rapid mood booster. The offering can additionally supply professional experience, social assistance, and networking opportunities.

Involve your family for assistance

Joblessness affects the entire household, so don't attempt to carry your troubles alone. Hiding your job loss from others will only complicate issues for you. Your family members' support can assist you in surviving and flourishing, also during this tough time.

Open to your family members.

Whether it's to relieve the stress or handle the sorrow of job loss, now is the time to lean on individuals that appreciate you, even if you take pride in being strong and self-dependent. Maintain them in the loop about your job search and tell them just how they can support you.

Pay attention to their problems.
Your members of the family are worried about you, in addition to their very own stability and future. Give them a chance to discuss their concerns and use tips concerning your employment search.

Make time for household fun.
Reserve normal household fun time where you can delight in each other's business, let off steam and forget about your unemployment troubles. This will help the entire family keep positive.

Face your feelings
Temper, depression, and stress and anxiety will certainly make it more challenging to get back on the job market, so it's important to manage your feelings and discover healthy methods to grieve proactively. It can be very easy to count on undesirable routines such as alcohol consumption way too much or bingeing on fast food for comfort. Yet these will just

supply short-lived relief and, in the lasting, make you really feel even worse. Acknowledging your feelings and challenging your unfavourable ideas, on the other hand, will certainly assist you in dealing with the loss and going on.

Pour out your expressions to trustworthy fellows

Express whatever you really feel regarding being laid off or jobless, consisting of things you wish you had stated (or had not stated) to your previous boss. This is especially cleansing if your discharge or discontinuation was handled in an insensitive method.

Approve fact

While it is essential to acknowledge exactly how challenging job loss and joblessness can be, it's similarly essential to prevent wallowing. Rather than dwelling on your job loss-- the unfairness; exactly how inadequately it was handled; the means you can have stopped it or how much far better life would be if it hadn't taken place-- attempt to accept the circumstance. The faster you do so, the earlier you can proceed with the next phase in your life.

Stay clear of beating yourself up

It's simple to start criticizing or condemning yourself when you've shed your job and are out of work. However, it is necessary to prevent putting yourself down. You'll require your self-esteem to remain intact as you're trying to find a new job. Challenge every unfavourable thought that experiences your head. If you begin to believe, "I'm a loser," make a note of evidence on the contrary: "I shed my job as a result of a firm takeover, not due to the fact that I misbehaved at my job."

Seek any kind of silver lining.

Shedding a job is easier to approve if you can locate the lesson in your loss. What can you learn from the experience? Perhaps your job loss and unemployment have provided you a possibility to reflect on what you desire out of life and reconsider your occupation top priorities. Possibly it's made you more powerful. If you look, you might be able to discover something of value.

Get relocating to relieve stress

If job dedications prevented you from working out frequently before, it's important to make the moment now. Along with relaxing, stressful muscles and soothing stress in the body, exercise launches powerful endorphins to improve your mood. Cutting your waistline and enhancing your figure may likewise offer your self-confidence an increase. Aim to work out for half an hour or even more each day, or break that up into brief, 10-minute bursts of activity. A 10- minute stroll can raise your spirits for two hours.

Rhythmic workout, where you relocate both your limbs, is an extremely reliable means to lift your state of mind, boost power, sharpen focus, and kick back both the body and mind. Try strolling, running, weight training, swimming, martial arts, or perhaps dancing.

Eat well to maintain your emphasis

Your diet plan may look like the last point you ought to problem yourself with when you're encountering the stress of job loss and unemployment. Yet what you place in your body can have a huge result on your degrees of power and positivity. Minimize sugar and fine-tuned carbs. You may crave sugary treats or home cooking such as pasta, white bread, potatoes, or French fries. However, these high-carbohydrate foods promptly cause an accident in mood and energy.

Avoid nicotine, Consume alcohol in small amounts. Alcohol may momentarily lower worry, yet way too much can create even higher stress and anxiety as it diminishes.

Take care of it on your own.
Currently, more than ever, it is very important to look after yourself. Maintain equilibrium in your life. Don't allow your job search to eat you. Make time for enjoyment, rest, and leisure, whatever renews you. Your job search will be extra efficient if you are emotionally, psychologically, and literally at your finest.

Obtain a lot of sleep.
Rest has a huge influence on your state of mind and efficiency. Ensure you're obtaining in between 7 to 8 hours of sleep every evening. It will assist you in maintaining your stress degrees controlled and keep your focus throughout your job search. Practice during your leisure methods. They additionally enhance your feelings of serenity and delight and educate you on how to stay tranquil and collected in difficult circumstances, including job interviews.

Keep favourable to maintain your power
If it's taking you longer than expected to locate work, the following ideas can assist you

to remain concentrated and upbeat. Maintain a routine day-to-day routine. Treat your job search like a job, with a day-to-day "begin" and "end" time, with normal times for workout and networking. Adhering to an established routine will aid you to be much more effective and productive.

Produce a job search plan. Prevent obtaining bewildered by damaging huge objectives into tiny, manageable actions as opposed to trying to do whatever priorities you have. Note your positives. Make a checklist of all the things you like concerning on your own, consisting of abilities, personality type, achievements, and successes. Make a note of projects you take pride in, scenarios where you stood out, and skills you have actually developed. Revisit this listing commonly to advise yourself of your stamina.

Find tasks that offer your life "definition." For many of us, our job provides our lives, indicating and function. Adhering to a job loss, it is very important to locate various other means to nourish your spirit. Pick up a long-neglected hobby, attempt a brand-new task, get associated with your community by offering or participating in local events, take a class, or join a club or sporting activities team.

Concentrate on what you can regulate. You can't control just how rapidly a possible employer calls you back or whether they choose to employ you. Rather than losing your priceless energy worrying about situations that are out of your hands, turn your attention to what you can regulate throughout your joblessness, such as finding out new abilities, composing a great cover letter and return to, and setting up meetings with your networking contacts.

Don't separate yourself

Complying with trauma, you might wish to withdraw from others, yet isolation only makes things worse. Attaching to others in person will certainly help you recover, so make an initiative to preserve your relationships and also prevent spending excessive time alone. You don't need to speak about the trauma. Connecting with others does not need to include speaking about the injury. Actually, for some individuals, that can just make things worse. Convenience originates from really feeling engaged and accepted by others.

CHAPTER 6 - Fixing damaged self-confidence

A certain period of time when you shed your positive self-image, and also self-worth can also be referred to as mojo. Your mojo is your idea in yourself, your vital force. You require your mojo. It is your fuel resource. It powers every little thing you do. Also, when your mojo gas tank seems to be full to the brim, you can lose most or all of your mojo instantaneously.

You might experience a Mojo Decrease since your job vanishes, or because you help a supervisor who berates and also slams you so much that you wind up doubting your abilities. The problem with a Mojo Decline is that individuals who have actually lost their mojo do not have a tendency to believe, "I'm great I have actually simply lost my mojo temporarily." They think simply the reverse: "I'm a loser! When I felt effective in the past that was just misconception. In fact, I'm not smart or qualified whatsoever!"

Lots of job-seekers and functioning people understand that their loss of self-worth isn't always logical or warranted, yet that expertise doesn't help quite. If you really feel a feeling, it is genuine for you! Knowing that your feelings do not make reasonable feeling is inadequate. You still feel them. During a Mojo Decline, lots of people really feel exhausted, dissuaded and self-critical.

Just how can you achieve your goals and have a happy life when your mojo is entirely gone? Just how can you job-hunt when your gas storage tank is vacant? You can't. You require to re-fill your mojo fuel storage tank, eventually at a time. Here are ten means to do it if these activities do not seem like company activities or beneficial methods to spend your time when you're "meant to" be job-hunting, offer yourself a break! Your fuel storage tank is your only source of power.

1. Nature is an excellent impact when you feel down or critical of yourself. In nature, we keep in mind that the universe is not against us. Life is everything about stages. It's tough, and however, when you enter your new character, things will certainly get better!

2. Obtain physical. Lift weights or dance to your favoured songs. Get out of your hectic brain and commemorate living by moving your body. Whatever you have performed in your life so far or have not done, you are still to life, and you can always change your circumstance!

3. Get creative. Pull out your paints and brushes or get involved in the garden and also design a blossom bed. Draw or write or play your viola. Your innovative brain is very important when you're in reinvention. It has messages for you. You will certainly feel much better when you allow yourself to re-connect with your innovative, non-linear side.

4. Get together with encouraging individuals. You recognize which buddies, associates, and family members make you feel light and also pleased. These are individuals to accompany now!

5. Talkback to your essential voice. Job-seekers, and individuals in reinvention, might have a nagging, important voice inside their heads frequently telling them how useless they are. Your important voice might state, "Why did you obtain laid off? Not every person in the department got given up. You must not have actually been a very good staff member!" You can debate to that important voice, either quietly, or out loud if there's no person around. State "Thanks for your opinion.

However, I can currently tell it's an advantage I got laid off. It's painful currently to be job-hunting. However, my following work is most likely to be far better than the last one. Unemployed as I am, my requirements are greater now!"

6. Just job-hunt for a couple of hours on a daily basis. That is the least reliable means to obtain work. Go out and have coffee with individuals you have actually known for several years and new individuals you've simply met. Sharing ideas and reinforcing one another is much better for your mojo gas container and your job search than treading through limitless application forms.

7. List your crucial Stories.
 You have powerful stories from your work and other areas of your life that will certainly remind you just how clever, qualified, and conscientious you are, however, only if you recall and reclaim them! Get a notepad and also start creating them down. Blog about the moments you conserved the day or really felt effective, and made a positive distinction. When our mojo disappears, and our self-esteem is fired, we tend to neglect our Dragon-Slaying Stories. You can do just the contrary, and make a checklist of them!

8. Clean your area and your mind. If you were functioning and then shed your job, you were possibly also hectic to organize your storage rooms. Do it now! Undergo your residence or home and eliminate garments you no more wear the furniture you're sick of and anything that does not sustain who you are currently and who you are becoming!

9. Imagine your following experience. You are not desperate, even if you feel desperate. Sit in a peaceful location and also picture your following journey. Create a vision in your mind. That vision will assist your mojo is returning, after all, that you can obtain thrilled about their future when they have no vision to pursue?

10. Ultimately, advise yourself how remarkable you are. In your head or aloud, tell on your own "This change is hard, but I'm going to come through it more powerful than I was previously. I know I'm clever and capable. The extra other individuals will feel it, as well!"

Individuals are typically confused regarding what it indicates to have self-esteem. Some assume it relates to the way you look or exactly how preferred you are with your good friends or others. Others think that having a wonderful body will aid you to get self-esteem, while others think you actually need to have completed something in order to have great self-esteem.

Come down to its simplicity. Self-esteem simply indicates appreciating on your own for that you are faults, characteristics, and all. It looks like other cultures don't face self-esteem as much as Americans do, maybe due to the emphasis, we seem to place on materialistic indicators of self-worth (like what sort of car you drive, what college your youngsters participate in, what your qualities are, exactly how large a home you have, or what your title goes to job).

The difference between somebody with healthy or good self-esteem and somebody who does isn't capability, per se. It's simply a recognition of your stamina and weaknesses and relocating through the world safe in that expertise.

Stop comparing yourself, absolutely nothing can injure our self-esteem greater than unreasonable contrasts. Joe has 3,000 Facebook pals while I only have 300. Mary can elude me on the field when we play ball. Elizabeth has a larger residence and a great auto than I do. You can see how this may impact our feelings about ourselves, the extra we do this kind of the point.

I know it is difficult. However, you require to stop comparing on your own to others. The only person you ought to be contending versus is yourself. These contrasts are unfair due to the fact that you don't know as much as you assume you do about these other individuals' lives or what it's really like to be them. You think it's better, but it may be 100 times worse than you can imagine.

CHAPTER 7 - Fixing love

When you think of it, every couple in every partnership is set up for failure. It's difficult to be mentally offered to your partner 100% of the time. However, failing is not trouble. Also, a mother that stopped working to be receptive and offered 50% of the time can increase a youngster to be a healthy adult with healthy partnerships. The difference between "good mommies and also poor mommies," according to Donald Winnicott, "is not the compensation of mistakes; however, what they finish with them."

Just how a child deals with everyday failings and fluctuations is directly pertaining to the level in which their parent develops an atmosphere for a safe accessory bond and just how that moms and dad repairs their mistakes.

This is no different in our enchanting relationships. The difference between pleasing couples and also dissatisfied couples is not that satisfied pairs don't make errors. All of us do exactly how pairs repair service is what divides the partnership Masters from the Catastrophes. The real distinction between the couples who repaired successfully and those who didn't was the psychological environment between partners.

Make positive deposits in your Emotional Savings Account by doing good things and valuing your companion. Your connection will certainly be a far better fit to stand the unpreventable tornados that will come if you are both an understanding of each other. If you are ill-mannered, disrespectful, and remote to each other after that, your repair work efforts will stop working. It's the high quality of the friendship that matters most in repairing the connection when things go wrong.

Repair services don't need to be well talked and even complicated to be effective. Any type of real strategy can work if a pair has the best foundation.

Despite what individuals tell you, melting bridges is a terrific means to keep up in the daily grind, dance in the flames of a burnt bridge is a wonderful inspiration to work faster and also keep pushing forward. However, sometimes you need to go back and restore a busted bridge for the much better good.

1. Start a Friendly and Polite Dialogue.
When you initiate a discussion, a simple "Hi there" or fast invite suffices. Just the truth that

you sent them a message may suffice, yet, relying on how they have actually blocked you, you might also require to state that you are. This is all that needs to be claimed, and also do not claim anything else (or send more than one total message) up until he or she responds, or you will certainly come off as frustrating.

2. Be Clear Concerning Your Intents.

As soon as there's a discussion open, utilize it for what it's worth being open, upfront, and honest concerning what you desire. This will signify to the other party that you appreciate him or her and also assist reconstruct the on what was previously broken. Never ever expect anyone to read your mind, due to the fact that the truth of the matter is, nobody can, regardless of how much you focus on transferring thoughts.

3. Love is All You Required.

The reason you're reconstructing a broken connection is due to the fact that you either need something or respect the person. Even if you need something, concentrate on the other person, not what you want.

4. Develop a Bridge, and for getting Over It.

Go down whatever concerns you used to have in the past. It's not the past anymore.

Bridge the gap in between both of you, and also get over your break with a quickness.

5. Be Honest (In a Great Way).

Always be truthful. Fraud may not have actually broken your relationship, yet it's certainly not most likely to fix it. Simply make certain you're neither protective nor offensive, and also, if you can't maintain it civil, shut up.

6. Brainstorming

Include the other individual in your efforts to reconstruct your partnership. If he or she is chatting, he or she is at the very least interested in hearing what you need to state, place the onus on them and request their payment.

7. Release Control.

Constantly keep in mind to remove on your own from the results in life. If you place all your eggs into his or she's basket, his/her denial will smash you. Instead, specify on your own and also how you respond, however, do not anticipate your optimal result.

8. Say sorry.

Learn to apologize. You just have to treat things as you do with terms and conditions on social media, you just scroll down and click on agreed without reading the contents. The same thing is applicable just say sorry for you to let peace reign.

9. Take Responsibility.

Always accept duty, even if you do not believe you were at fault. The various other individuals plainly think you are, and approving responsibility, will certainly aid you to bridge the gap between your assumptions.

10. Prevent Pushing Buttons.

Bear in mind that both you and the various other events have bitterness toward each other (or a minimum of utilized to). You know there are particular triggers that get to that individual be a grown-up and prevent pushing those buttons, no matter how badly you're tempted.

11. Believe Favourable.

It's always a great suggestion to assume favourable in life. Even if things don't exercise, you can believe positively concerning the following experience. Maintain looking forward, and also you'll show self-confidence, which is attractive to other people. This will certainly attract the various other people to ask yourself why she or he does not have a connection with you.

12. Be Genuine.

Always be the actual you, regardless of what happens. You prefer to fail your method than succeed as somebody else. Never mind acting to be what the various other person wants. It's not a competitor, and also you would certainly be amazed at how much honesty will open doors for you in life.

13. Impose Your Limits.

You have individual limits, and you're heading out of your method not to overstep other individuals' borders, so you are entitled to regard also. Make certain to pleasantly and also carefully advise the other individual whenever they have actually violated a border you established. However, make sure it's one you've both recognized exists, so you're not wrongly charging anybody of crossing a line he or she really did not understand was there.

14. Sometimes You Need To Let Go.

Regardless of your best purposes, there's an opportunity the various other people simply don't wish to reconnect. There are billions of individuals in the world, and there's definitely no factor to lose your time on one who does not like you. Restoring a busted relationship is hard. Both parties need to encounter the displeasure and suspect that drove you apart in the first place. If you're aim to resolved a damaged affairs from your past, reconnect with the person with text, email, or online.

CHAPTER 8 - How to repair a heart after beign broken.

We have all had our hearts broken. When it happens to you personally, it's devastating, and while people can associate, they aren't because of a minute. The pain is there, and it's actual for you. Sometimes it feels like you're totally helpless, and you'll never ever surpass the suffering. The important things to bear in mind are that there are people there for you, which there is constantly light at the end of the passage. You need to understand that getting over a break up appears unachievable, but it's almost the issue of time.

Steps to Adhere To:

1. Cut all the contact.
This truth is regulation in a separate. Maintain your distance and do not text, e-mail, fulfil in person, or phone call. You should most likely take them off your Facebook or any other socials media while you go to it. This doesn't have to be irreversible, but while you're at risk of any kind of mean or, on the other hand, loving words, it's ideal not to have their voice in your head.

The danger of getting back into a connection when it had not been working is high. You might likewise end up in a battle of words causing further pain and stress and anxiety. Cutting the connections completely when it more than puts you on a much faster course to recovery.

2. Let Your Feelings Out.

Cry, sob your eyes out, shout and shout. As long as it doesn't harm yourself or anyone else, discover means to launch and let go of the pain you might be feeling. When individuals kindly and humorously tell you all separate is hard, it's due to the fact that they are. You will naturally feel some adverse emotions, no matter just how easy or tough your separation was. Honour your sensations and know that they will certainly obtain less intense the much more that you let them out. It assists you to pass them!

3. Accept the reality that it more than, at least in the meantime.

Dealing with completion of a partnership is a little like a 12 step program. You will reach acceptance far sooner by steering clear of from that individual. This technique counts on time greater than anything else, but there are ways to move it along. Attempt to look at the circumstance fairly, even if you really did not accept the break-up. Do not over-analyse what can have been different. There are unlimited should-haves and could-haves, and thinking about them will create you to spiral.

In the minutes you were in the relationship, your reactions do matter a lot. They don't any longer. Your mission currently is to get to the location where you aren't coping yourself concerning the means things are. Do this with empathy and also don't defeat on your own up going.

4. Find Yourself

Chances are you shed a piece of yourself in the connection. Currently, it is your opportunity to find you again, and also this can be fun. This is among the positives to your break up, so accept it! Perhaps you let go of a pastime you made use of to enjoy to do or quit taking perfumed bathrooms. You can eat salad and also granola bars for supper if you seem like it. There is plenty of personal things that made you special, and you just have to discover them again and also get the sensation back.

Conversely, you may have grown in the partnership, which indicates you can uncover brand-new things about on your own.

5. Discover and Have Fun.

When you prepare to authentically enjoy again, obtain your partners together and head out. Go dance, shop, take place a roller rollercoaster. Do something that makes you smile, laugh, and really feel excellent within. I once went to a haunted home where things leaped out at me and terrified me half to fatality. This was so healing. Be spontaneous and also foolish. Enjoy your life.

6. Give Your Thoughts some attention

As you aim to proceed in your life, do not reject or understand your ex-lover's memory. They may stand out into your mind as a memory of a minute where you enjoyed (or otherwise). Recognize it, grin, or sob. Allow the memory to go instead of clinging onto it. Do not intentionally check out photos or take a look at old messages you obtained from him. It now concerns you and your present moments. Your ex-lover is a part of the person you are today, and also, you can be thankful to them for that. However, the phase with them is gone.

7. Don't rush into an additional partnership.

Don't jump right into one more relationship too swiftly, believing that you're alright. It is possibly the best quick fix out there, but at the same time, you never really overcome your ex. Over time you haven't actually overcome your ex-spouse, and when your following relationship ends, you'll have two ex's to get over. You're just lengthening the inevitable pain.

8. Develop a mindful life.

It's good to gradually and progressively create a conscious life so your mind can stay tranquil and tranquil whatever life throws you. Being conscious means, you pay attention to yourself even more and acknowledge you're most significantly, comprehend what can make you happy.

CHAPTER 9 - Healing with nature

Our link with nature is basic to our wellness and health. The lives of our forefathers were elaborately linked with nature, and several societies sought to the planet for knowledge and recovery. It might appear evident that nature is very important, yet many individuals in this globe are entirely nature-deprived, and scientific research is hectic attempting to discuss why, precisely, we require it a lot.

Currently, researchers are presenting inquiries that can just be pondered by contemporary people like discovering just how you really feel when you watch out your home window at a concrete wall surface contrasted to a stunning field, sea, or sundown. If you were to think of these two situations, today, I'm quite certain you would certainly discover a distinction in exactly how your body responds. So is it any type of question our bodies respond in a different way of being bordered by a concrete jungle versus being out in the marvels of nature?

If there is a distinction in exactly how you really feel when it pertains to considering nature from your home window, picture just how favourable the results are when you are really submersing your detects in nature in real-time when you're really feeling the wind touch your skin, the sunlight heating your body, the smell of the sea air, or the preference of sea salt on your lips. I wager you discovered your body start to loosen up by the simple summaries of an experience in nature.

Once more, if considering nature or checking it out through the home window brings about favourable modifications in our state of mind and the stress you're keeping in your body, envision exactly how valuable it, in fact, is to be IN nature, and alternatively how damaging it can be to your wellness to be empty or divided from nature.

People advanced elaborately attached to nature for countless years. The nomadic life of searching and celebration quit just around 10,000 years earlier when farming took control of, and also after that, our forefathers endured of residences made from the planet and consumed foods straight expanded from the planet. They took a trip without vehicles or innovation and recovered the unwell with wild natural herbs. They would certainly climb with the sunlight and retire with the sundown with the celebrities overhanging leading their method.

Innovation has actually taken control of, side-tracking us from our demand to be outdoors or attached to nature. And though it has actually enabled lots of extraordinary developments in wellness, it has actually likewise maintained us from being attached to something that we, as humans, require in our lives to really feel ideal.

Can nature actually make you better?

Researches verify that nature resembles a decrease of morphine in mind, promoting the launch of feel-good chemicals like dopamine, which assist you really feel better. As an example, research performed in Korea revealed individuals pictures of country versus metropolitan scenes.

They located that there was a raised task in the former temporal post, the part of the mind that is connected with adverse feelings, actions, and feelings like temper and clinical depression in reaction to the metropolitan scenes. However, when the individuals checked out the country images, there was much more task in the incentive locations of the mind like the basic ganglia and dopaminergic benefit facilities, which are connected with psychological security, compassion, love, delighted memories and enjoyment. These coincide locations of the mind that represent delighted faces and recollection of delighted memories.

Nature recovery power.

Scientific research and pop culture might quickly be beginning to value something that you have actually likely understood for a very long time remaining in natural positive effect to the body.

It comes as not a surprise to listen to that being outdoors in the timbers, bordered by living, breathing plants, birds, and pets, can reduce your stress and anxiety degrees, boost your state of mind and battle clinical depression, boost your memory, and boost your basic feeling of health if you're strolling and obtaining your heart price up, all the much better. Though many of us have actually intuited or straight experienced these advantages ourselves, clinical study and publications regarding the topic get on the surge.

For the very first time in the background, even more individuals throughout the globe stay in cities than in backwoods. Even more, people invest our days inside in atmospheres lacking all-natural impact. Integrated with the fast increase of modern technology in our day-to-day lives, from computer systems and television to pads and smart devices, a growing number of individuals have actually restricted time, gain access to, and wish to experience the environment.

Currently, some individuals are moving their emphasis from subordinate direct exposure to nature to proactively looking for the possible recovery residential or commercial properties of the environment. The Japanese have actually been advertising the advantages of hanging out in woodlands for years. A preferred method in Japan, called Shinrin-yoku, which equates to forest-bathing, is the wilful procedure of taking in the views, scents, and audios of an all-natural set up to make the best use of physical and psychological wellness.

Those people that recognize and enjoy the landscapes of western Massachusetts will likely not be amazed by any one of these patterns or researches. The timbers, rivers, and ranches we are fortunate to see, stroll, or go to often have actually profited our bodies and minds in methods we might knowingly value, or possibly we just recognize we like being outdoors in this unique area.

Will the environment-friendly room decrease your anxiety degrees?

Several research studies verify that whether a person is submerged in nature, considering nature, or thinking of nature, there is far better recuperation from stress and anxiety, much less task in the amygdala (the concerned facility in the mind), reduced degrees of stress and anxiety hormonal agents like cortisol, and reduces in high blood pressure, heart price, and muscle mass stress. Additionally, evidently, the much more environment-friendly room you live alongside, the much better you go to recuperating from tension as if the environment-friendly area functions as a real stress-buffering system.

Can nature aid you in restoring your wellness after ailment or injury?

It shows up that whether you're taking a look at an attractive sight of nature, are seen by a pet dog, or have a plant in the area, nature aids you recover, really feel much less nervous, have much less pain, have much more power, and leave the medical facility quicker.

Will getting in touch with the world boost your mental health and wellness?

If you resemble me, investing way too much time in front of the display leaves me with mind haze and tiredness. Alternatively, being out in nature leaves me feeling alert and stimulated to ensure that I have actually boosted emphasis and focus. Seems acquainted? Well, scientific research verifies that this is, in fact, real for the majority of people, revealing that direct exposure to nature can enhance interest, power, memory, state of mind, and cognition.

For instance, it has actually been revealed that individuals that stroll in the woodland versus a city setting have considerable renovations in cognition after the stroll, and trainees that have an unhampered sight of nature outmatch their peers that do not have this sight on standard steps of focus. When it comes to kids with ADHD, the greenness of the backyard has actually been connected with milder signs and symptoms of focus shortage, and windowless interior backyard has actually been related to much more serious signs.

Is exterior work-out the very best sort of workout?

For lots of people, the workout is a task. Nevertheless, it appears that being outdoors makes workout less complicated. So whether you're running or strolling, doing it out in nature rather than inside your home has actually been connected with even more power, and much less exhaustion, pain, and negative attitude. For professional athletes, this is likewise real. Scientists at Texas State

College, for instance, discovered that professional athletes' efficiencies boosted when they were bordered by even more eco-friendly area.

There is insecurity and likewise, instability, concealed by perfectionism and likewise constantly aiming to be the very best, at every little thing. There is hurting solitude behind the grinning face that you think secures you. There is stress and anxiety that the globe you're managing will certainly come collapsing down, and likewise, your susceptibility will certainly be revealed. So you realize a lot more snugly to the photo and likewise "good life" you have actually produced.

The much better the life you have actually appeared to produce, the extra you can really feel the stress to maintain the exterior. The even more ideal the life others regard you to have, the more challenging you might feel you need to function to preserve that picture. It's continuous. It's an important ability in life to concentrate on the favourable, no question regarding it. You can bring an advantage also means much. You can stay clear of, price cut, and likewise reject anything agonizing.

Currently, when it would certainly be appropriate and likewise healthy and balanced for you to really feel those feelings, you have a hard time to access them due to the fact that you have actually concealed them away so well, and they are maintaining you from taking part in life completely.

It really feels if you do, you'll never quit weeping, or your craze will certainly eat you. If you do not, you'll never completely live. You will certainly quit sobbing. Your temper will certainly discolour.

Yes, you need to welcome life in its whole, pain consisted of. There are publications and likewise films and likewise photos and likewise all kind of brand-new types of contemporary art, such as efficiencies, that take care of pain. They have the power to pass through deep right into the artists' and likewise the target market's hearts. They irreversibly transform us permanently.

Can getting in touch with nature enhance your body's immune system?

Nature assists you feel better, yet it additionally aids you in improving. One factor for this originates from hidden components in nature called phytoncides, which aid reduced stress and anxiety hormonal agents, stress and anxiety, and pain along with boost the manufacturing of anti-cancer healthy proteins in the blood and the front-line immune-defence natural-killer cells.

Various other undetected aspects consist of the tiny adversely billed ions that are located in tidy air; these have actually been revealed to help in lowering tension and stress and anxiety and enhancing cognitive efficiency, injury recovery, and antioxidant task. These adverse ions are promptly diminished in contaminated settings, confined and cool spaces, and specifically spaces that have digital tools such as computer systems, copy machines, and televisions. Unfavourable ions are extra plentiful in all-natural setups, after rain, near seas and fall, and inside ache woodlands and forests.

Are you persuaded yet? The study is plentiful, and there are a lot of research studies to mention whether they're indicating the advantages of sunshine or consuming even more environment-friendlies on how you can make use of nature to restore your wellness. The bright side is that it is very easy to obtain nature back right into your life, even if you reside in a city setup.

How You Can Get In Touch With Nature

1. Maintain pictures of nature around you.

Even if you cannot go out in nature, you can invest time valuing images of nature. Maintain them spread around your office or home forever step.

2. Stroll.

Feeling worried? Opt for a stroll in a yard, the coastline, or in a grassy field packed with blossoms. Involve every one of your minds and truly enjoys the experience.

3. Workout exterior.

Discover areas to work out in nature. Discover a park, woodland, or coastline, as an example. If you select to stroll, do so for a minimum of 20 minutes.

4. Practice mindfulness out in nature.

Involve all your minds in the here and now minute, valuing the noises, views, scents, preferences, and feel of whatever around you. Check out every little thing in nature with wonder. Attempt to do this technique for at the very least 20 minutes.

5. Pay attention to directed reflections that include scenes of nature.

Feel-good chemicals will certainly move with your mind and body both due to the fact that you are practicing meditation and firing up memories of remaining in nature.

6. Do a weekend break vacation in a natural setup.

Eliminating on your own from your everyday anxiety and submersing on your own in nature will certainly do marvels for your anxiety degrees and psychological wellbeing. In the olden days, physicians made use of to recommend "eco-friendly" treatment to their clients to locate their calmness, peace of mind, and health and wellness. Pick an area that is attractive where you have the chance to check out nature or merely rest silently in it.

7. Consume in such a way that links you with nature.

Consume foods that normally expand from the planet, ideally natural, from neighbourhood ranches, or from your very own yard. The closer you feel to the food you consume, the closer you feel to the planet, and the much healthier you will certainly be.

8. Grow your very own yard.

Farm and watch greenery expand from seed to fruit or veggie. Your link with on your own, the planet, and life itself will certainly be improved. Investing that time outdoors will certainly additionally supply you a little workout, vitamin D, and a lot of feel-good nature treatment.

9. Direct exposure on your own to adverse ions.

Obtain outside after rain and absorb the adverse ions and placed plants throughout your home and workplace to bring nature right into your house. If you go to a job or in your home and are having a tough time focusing, take a fast nature break. Go with a stroll, take in revitalizing air, or rest silently by a tree or natural landscape if you can.

CHAPTER 10 - Repairing your joy

Every now and then, I fulfil a person that emits joy. These are people that seem to radiance with an internal light. They are kind, serene, thrilled by tiny enjoyments, and thankful for the huge ones. These individuals are not the best. They get tired and stressed. They make mistakes in judgment. However, they live for others and not for themselves. They understand why they were put on this planet and acquire a deep complete satisfaction from doing what they have been contacted us to do.

Life isn't simple for these people. They've tackled the worries of others. But they have a peacefulness concerning them, and worked-out willpower. They have an interest in you, make you really feel valued and known, and like your good.

When you fulfil these people, you realize that delight is not just a sensation it can be an expectation. There are short-lived highs most of us get after we win some victory, and then there are various other kinds of permanent happiness that animate individuals who are not consumed with themselves. However, they have actually given themselves away. I usually find that their life has what I think of as a two-mountain shape.

They got out of the institution, began their job or began a family, and recognized the hill they assumed they were indicated to climb: I'm going to be a police, a physician, and an entrepreneur, what have you.

On the very first mountain, most of us have to perform certain life jobs: develop an identification that is different from our parents, grow our abilities, build a secure ego and try to make a mark in the world. Individuals climbing that very first mountain spend a lot of time thinking of credit monitoring. They are constantly maintaining scores. How do I measure up? Where do I rank? As the psychotherapist James Hollis puts it, at that stage, we tend to think, "I am what the world states I am."

The objectives on that initial hill are the normal goals that our culture endorses to be a success, to be well considered, to obtain welcomed right into organisations. It's all the regular stuff: wonderful home, wonderful family, good holidays, great food, friends and so forth.

Some people succeed in that very first hill, taste success, and find it unsatisfying. They notice there has to be a much deeper journey they can take. Other people obtain ripped off that hill by some failing. Something happens to their profession, their family, or their online reputation. Suddenly life does not appear like a steady ascent up the hill of success; it has a different and more unsatisfactory shape.

For others, something unanticipated takes place that knocks them crossways: the death of a child, cancer cells scare, a struggle with dependency, some life-altering catastrophe that was not part of the original plan. Whatever the reason, these individuals are no longer on the mountain.

These seasons of enduring have a way of exposing the under surfaces of ourselves and reminding us that we're not individuals we thought we were. There is one more layer to them they have actually been disregarding, a substratum where the dark injuries and most effective yearnings live.

Some shrivel in the face of this sort of suffering. They appear to obtain even more worried and much more resentful. They reduce far from their internal depths in worry. Their lives lessen and lonelier. We all understand old people who registered nurse timeless grievances. They do not obtain the respect they are entitled to. They live their lives as an endless outburst concerning some wrong done to them long ago.

But for others, this valley is the production of them. The period of enduring disrupts the surface flow of day-to-day life. They see deeper into themselves and realize that down in the substratum, moving from all the tender places, there is a basic ability to care, a yearning to transcend the self and care for others. And when they have actually experienced this yearning, they are ready to come to be an entire individual.

They see acquainted things with brand-new eyes. They are ultimately able to enjoy their next-door neighbours as themselves, not as a motto; however, a useful fact. Their life is specified by just how they react to their minute of best misfortune.

Individuals who are made larger by suffering take place to organize two tiny disobediences. Initially, they rebel versus their ego suitable. When they got on their initial hill, their vanity had some vision of what it was shooting for some vision of prestige, satisfaction, and success. Down in the valley, they dislike their vanity perfect. Of course, later, they still feel and sometimes succumb to their selfish wishes.

Second, they start to rebel versus conventional culture. All the lives they have actually been residing in a society that shows that human beings pursue self-involvement cash, power, fame. Yet instantly, they are not interested in what other individuals tell them to desire. They wish to want things that are truly worth desiring.

They raise their desires. The globe tells them to be an excellent customer, yet they wish to be the one eaten by an ethical reason. The world tells them to want independence. However, they desire connection to be snared in a web of warm connections.

The world tells them to desire individual freedom. However, they desire intimacy, duty, and dedication. The globe desires them to rise and pursue success, but they intend to be an individual for others. The magazines on the publication rack want them to ask, "What can I do to make myself delighted?" but they glance something bigger than individual joy. Besides, There's one bigger mountain out there that is, my hill." The 2nd mountain is not the opposite of the very first hill. To climb, it doesn't imply denying the very first hill. It's the journey after it. It's a more generous and satisfying stage of life and it can occur at any kind of age.

Conclusion

With our professions and personal lives, we experience cheerful heights and painful valleys. The latter can cover a variety of difficult situations, be it a major expert error, a distressing health problem, or an ongoing fight with our problems. The Japanese viewpoint of Kintsugi offers an informative perspective to help us cope with such scenarios. From the Kintsugi point of view, the damages aren't implied to be concealed like new.

Actually, the damage and repair include value, offering the brought back things a distinct background and appeal it did not have in the original. Busted things are approved where they are and still seen as worthwhile of care, as opposed to being discarded as inferior. Failing isn't the end of the roadway; it's a step along a lot longer journey.

When we anticipate every little thing and everybody to be best, including ourselves, we not just discount rate much of what is beautiful but we develop a harsh globe where sources are squandered, people's favourable top qualities are ignored in favour of their defects, and our standards become impossibly limiting, restrictive, and unhealthy.

Kintsugi educates us to steer clear of all self-defeating psychological verdicts, the "stories" we have actually built concerning just how difficult it is for us to recuperate from our destruction, dishonesties, and losses. It raises our self-esteem and informs us that there is no embarrassment in getting beat or having irreparable downsides.

Kintsugi is all about changing emphasis from what's currently shed, to what's been obtained. From broken too changed. From much less to extra. It tells us to recognize our experiences since when we begin doing that, we recognize it's only the splinters, nicks, swellings & breaks in your life that include worth to it.

You can also think about sharing your journey with others. Research reveals that we tend to judge our very own failures a lot more harshly than other individuals, which might make you resistant to assert the adverse parts of your life tale.

The idea of accepting imperfection is also very closely connected to credibility, which makes you a far better leader. In the Kintsugi worldview, unbroken ceramic isn't special; all of it looks the same, without defining qualities. Your lines of those precious scars are what make you unique, and sharing them with others enables you to forge much deeper, extra engaging relationships and be happy once again in your life.

Printed in Great Britain
by Amazon